Coaches'

Practice Guide

Drills, skills, games and more to help you get through
your *youth girls' lacrosse* practice!

Kate Leavell

NOW INCLUDES COACHES GUIDE 2.0!!!!

LeavellUp
16441 Jarreau Ct
Lakeville MN 55044

www.kateleavell.com

Ordering Information:
Quantity sales. Special discounts are available on quantity purchases by corporations, associations, and others. For details, contact the publisher at the address above.
Orders by U.S. trade bookstores and wholesalers. Please contact kate@kateleavell.com

Printed in the United States of America

Publisher's Cataloging-in-Publication data
Leavell, Katherine.
Coaches Emergency Practice Guide / Kate Leavell

ISBN: 978-1-329-53720-0

2nd Addition 2017 Printed with additional Bonus Material

For my kids who support me in every coaching job, even when it means they will be dragged along to practice or eating pizza AGAIN, my husband who stood by me and my lacrosse obsession so much that he finally became a referee and a coach himself so that we could be together more, to my fellow CDP trainers who inspire me and always have the best insights to the game, to Debbie- the best assistant coach I ever had, and to an amazing person who introduced himself to me in an airport and then encouraged me to be so much more than I ever knew I could be – thank you Jon Gordon.

Love you guys, this was not possible without you!

Also by Kate Leavell: **Confessions of an Imperfect Coach**

An experiment in team culture that changed everything.

Navigate the GUIDE

Coaches'

Emergency

Practice Guide

Even the best coaches can struggle when teaching an age group that is unfamiliar. Sometimes that last minute, seemed like a good idea at the time, sure I can help with the kindergarten team or coach my kids team in my spare time, commitment can be a little more challenging than we thought.

Having a coaching emergency? As a coaching education trainer, the biggest request I get is for drills and progressions for various age groups, fun games, and appropriate skills suggestions for youth players. I knew the thirty plus notebooks of drills I have compiled over the years and the countless youth clinics I've put on would come in handy one day, and you now get the benefit. On your way to the field with no practice plan? No worries, I've got ya covered!!

No more worrying about getting your players motivated, when the drills are fun they engage more at practice, which means they learn more, and everyone wins! Grab some quick tips, last minute game and ice breaker ideas, and drill progressions and have a great practice that hopefully leaves your players learning, having a blast and ready to come back for more!

And **Thank YOU** for giving your time to develop our youth athletes. It's because of caring coaches like yourself, that our kids are gaining the life lessons, confidence, skills, and physical abilities that they will benefit from throughout their lives.

Kate Leavell

Girls Lacrosse

Developing Youth

Players

Development

GOAL at the youth stage:

Introduce basic body movements needed to play sports, introduce the lacrosse stick and the fundamental skills of holding and using the stick. Introduce safety concepts, as well as working with others as a team in small groups. Physical fitness and body awareness, instilling a love of physical activity and sports through perceived success individually as well as valued contribution within a team environment.

Skills to be introduced:

- Cutting – changing speed and direction
- Pivoting – using the correct foot, turning the right way, getting low, pushing off
- Jumping, leaping, skipping
- Balance
- Hand eye coordination
- Decision making
- Aerobic Conditioning
- Communicating
- Teamwork
- Listening and comprehension
- Basic Stick-work, hand positioning, for cradle, catch, throw, and scoop
- Basic rules and field lines (crease, boundaries, freeze on whistle, safety points)
- Body positioning – defensive stance, stick protection and triple threat, etc)
- Introduce team tactics, build progressions as they learn

Teaching Techniques:

- Focus on one piece of a skill at a time
- Use demonstration and then allow them to try it
- Ask questions instead of giving answers to get them thinking
- Praise effort, encourage risking failure
- Build slowly, give them time to master each piece separately first
- If they don't understand, break it down further
- Turn it into a game, a song, or a challenge.
- They will be as excited about doing it as you are about presenting it

Special Considerations for Youth Players:

- Children have trouble regulating temperature, they will become hotter and dehydrated faster than older kids and adults. They will get colder extremities and frost bite faster.
- Attention spans are very short, use short sentences and get to the point quickly. Use buzz words and phrases instead of long paragraphs.
- They learn visually and by doing the best. Walk them through the drill, let them try it in slow motion, draw a picture or use props to demo it if possible.
- Keep lines as short as possible, bored kids are hard to redirect once you lose their attention. Great rule of thumb is no more than 3 in a drill or line. Make stations of 3 and walk around from station to station. When possible, give every kid a ball and have them do it at the same time to avoid any down time.
- Layer work with fun. For example: Intro skill, do a drill to practice it, then do a short fun activity, take a break and then repeat with a different skill.
- For example: Intro dodging basics with giant steps around cones. Have them dodge a partner, then play tag where they can practice dodging to get across the field.
- It's ok if it's ugly. The drills won't look good most of the time. You know a drill is successful if it has the following 3 things:
  1. All of the kids are engaged, little to no standing around
  2. The kids are motivated to put effort into the drill, its challenging enough to work hard, but realistic enough that they can find success if they try hard.
  3. There is an element of fun mixed in with the learning.
- Keep the focus on what you would like the players to do, eliminate DON'T from your vocabulary.
- Look for genuine reasons to praise often, let them feel pride in their efforts rather than a focus on outcomes.
- Learn their names, it means a lot to a kid when the coach learns their names.
- Try not to expect it to look much like lacrosse at this point. They are still learning to use their bodies and their fine motor skills are a few years off.
- At the youngest ages, cutting down sticks to a manageable length is helpful. Making the pocket larger for more successful catching is also helpful. Using light weight balls helps instill confidence with less fear. (tennis balls, pinky balls, raquet balls, Swax balls, etc) But at the middle school age, players need a full size pole in order to have reach for defense and leverage for shooting, throwing, drawing, and grabbing passes.

BUZZ Words and Phrases

(Vocab words that spark a quick reminder to act out a skill.)

Ground Balls:
Knuckles to Grass
Both Butts Down
Trace the Upside Down Rainbow (down, push through, back up)
Go Fish (down into the water, catch a fish, bring the fish back up)

Throwing:
Show off your muscles! (to get rid of chicken wing and push throws)
Tray (hold the stick up and flat like a tray on your top hand)
Camera ready! (point the imaginary camera in the butt end of the stick at your partner when you are getting ready to throw and also at the end of a catch)
Put it in your back pocket! (getting the bottom hand across the body after pulling)
Look at your watch! (getting bottom hand up and elbow away from the body like trying to see a watch on the bottom hand)

Catching:
Target (Put the head of the stick up and ask for it where you want them to throw it too)
Jello arms (relaxed hands and arms to slow the ball down gently rather than batting at it)
Drop Step (dropping the dominant foot back as they catch to help reinforce soft hands)
Laser Beams (keeping laser beams from the eyes on the ball until its safe in the stick's pocket)
Don't break the egg (reminder for relaxed arms and gentle movements)

Field Markings and Rules:
Hot Coals! The area inside the 8 meter. It's hot in there, if you don't move through quickly you burn your feet. Defenders only protect feet if they are close enoughto touch an offense player.
First 7 people to the party! Last 4 house sit! Reminder that after 7 people cross the restraining line, 4 people plus the goalie must stay back.
Bobble Heads: keep head on a swivel looking left and right while running to know whats going on and be prepared to change direction or pass the ball.

Different Kinds of Players (and how to deal)

The needy player: this is the one that hangs on your legs, is always front and center and so close you can't move, sometimes this is the one that cries frequently at practice. Needy players well…need something. You get to choose what they receive, not the other way around. Give them constant tasks, they can set up cones, check the net for holes, carry balls. Eventually the needy player may start receding to the background to stop getting picked for all the chores ☺

The distractor: Similar to the needy player, this child is seeking attention. Throw your attention heavily onto other players who are acting appropriately and then when the distractor attempts to get your attention positively, let them have an appropriate amount of praise and then immediately move on. If this doesn't work, during a drill pull the player aside and have a positive talk about how you wonder if they could help you keep the team focused and do they have any ideas of what being focused looks like.

The I don't want to participate at anything-er: There's always one. If you have more than one, I feel your pain. These kids often need a personal invitation to do everything. If they don't engage after trying to pull them in several times, ask them one on one, what sort of things they enjoy and then try to relate those things somehow to practice skills. Keep encouraging and making some one on one effort. Ask some of the stronger more confident players to partner with them and mentor them.

The Faker: I broke my ankle this morning, my stomach hurts, last night a twisted my neck bones so I can't run…. These are just another source of attention seeking, but with the added complication of legally – we can't assume they are faking on the off chance they may actually be injured or ill. A quick – oh that sounds awful, will you be just watching practice today? Will usually clear up any fake injuries and if not when the parents arrive to pick them up you can explain that they were feeling too ill or injured to participate. Try to avoid letting them just sit out for running and then letting them back in for drills unless you know they have something like asthma that requires a longer break.

The Complainer: A strict no complaining rule should be set up at the beginning of the season. If anyone has a suggestion for better options, they can bring them to you on a piece of paper at the end or beginning of the next practice. If they don't like something they are challenged to come up with one positive thing they can get out of it anyway. Praise those positive thoughts thoroughly!

Games,
Ice Breakers,
And FUN!

For all youth age levels

The Stick Game:
Skills (hand eye coordination, listening, reaction time, sportsmanship)

Gather the girls into a circle, they will need their sticks for this activity. They should be pretty close together with just enough room to move around in their own space. Have the players hold their sticks UPSIDE DOWN with the head on the ground and using two fingers on the butt of the stick to keep it upright. On the coaches' signal, the girls will move at the same time, letting go of their stick and moving to grab the stick of the person on their right. If they are unable to grab the stick and it falls and hits the ground then they are out. At this age, it's easier to keep moving in the same direction every time. Allow for several practice rounds. The players may not throw their own stick down in order to keep someone else from grabbing it. As there are less people in the game, have the players take a giant step backwards after each elimination as well as slide around to fill in any large gaps in the circle. The last three and then two players stand back to back, they step forward each round until there is only one player left. This game takes approximately 10-15 minutes to set up and complete for a team sized group.

Lax Knock Out:

Skills (hand eye coordination, stick awareness, peripheral vision, cardio, strategy, scooping, cradling, stick protection)

Put the players inside either the center circle on the field or a circle made from cones. You can also use any random lines on your field or gym floor that can contain the players and provide a boundary. Players will each have their own ball in their stick. At the coaches signal they will move around inside the area trying to protect their stick as well as using one hand to try to knock the ball out of someone else's stick. If they drop the ball on their own at this age, allow them to scoop it back up and only count it as out if someone else knocks their ball down. Once a player's ball has been knocked out they can either be out of the game or you can give them a number to count to before being allowed back into the circle to try again.

Hungry Hungry Hippos:
Skills (Ground balls, cradling, time pressure, competition, sportsmanship)

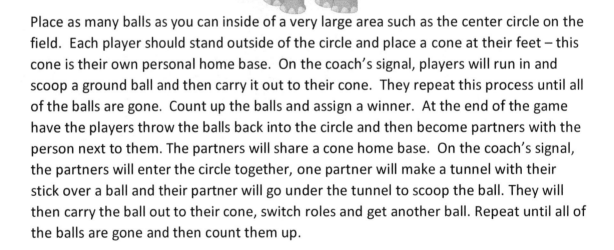

Place as many balls as you can inside of a very large area such as the center circle on the field. Each player should stand outside of the circle and place a cone at their feet – this cone is their own personal home base. On the coach's signal, players will run in and scoop a ground ball and then carry it out to their cone. They repeat this process until all of the balls are gone. Count up the balls and assign a winner. At the end of the game have the players throw the balls back into the circle and then become partners with the person next to them. The partners will share a cone home base. On the coach's signal, the partners will enter the circle together, one partner will make a tunnel with their stick over a ball and their partner will go under the tunnel to scoop the ball. They will then carry the ball out to their cone, switch roles and get another ball. Repeat until all of the balls are gone and then count them up.

The Great Race

Skills: (ground balls on the move, teamwork, speed, time pressure)

Make several lines of players. Each line is a team working together. Each player should be about 5-10 yards in front of the player behind them on their team if you have enough space. Place a pile of balls at the front of each line. Make sure each pile has the same number of balls. On the coach's signal, the first player in each line will go to their pile, scoop a ground ball and roll it to the next player on their team. That player will scoop the ball coming at them and then turn and roll it to the player behind them. This repeats until the ball is to the last player in line who will start to form a pile. As soon as the first ball is rolled, the first player will go get another ball so that many balls are working their way through the line at once. Once all the balls are piled up at the end of the line, the team starts again, working the balls back to a pile in the front of the line. When they are all piled up back in the front of the line the team sits down and puts their stick in the air to signal being done. Rules: balls must be rolled and not thrown, it must be a legal scoop without raking. Each player in line must scoop it, if it rolls past a player they must go get it, take it back to their spot and then roll it to the next person. They must scoop it completely and cannot just bat at the ball to keep it moving.

Cradle Wars:
Skills (stick awareness, hand eye coordination, teamwork, ground balls)

Divide the group into teams, line them up at the beginning of the field or gym in relay race style. Give each player a ball. The first person in line will run to the cone placed out ahead of them while trying not to drop the ball in their stick (they do not have to cradle but they can't hold the ball in the stick with anything). When they get back to their line they will use their stick to transfer their ball into the next person's stick who will now have two balls to transport around the cones. If they drop the balls while they are running they may only put one ball back into their stick. When they get back they will transfer with their stick both balls (or only one if they were dropped) into the next persons stick. This keeps going until all of the players on each team have gone. Award teams points for coming in first, second, etc. Then award teams points for how many balls they had in their stick when the last person arrives back in line.

Lava Bridge Race
Skills (Conditioning, balance, following instructions, body awareness, spacing, critical thinking, teamwork)

Using the lines on the field/gym, create an adventure race for your players. Split your group into two or three teams. Have the teams come up with a name and then appoint a team leader. Using the lines on the field or the gym, come up with an obstacle race. Assign a place on the field as the goal that each team is trying to get too. Each color of lines should represent an activity and they must use the lines to get to the end point. For example, all the blue lines mean you must hop on one foot, red lines mean crawl, black lines are skipping, etc. They can follow the lines any way they want to find the end point but they must not step off the lines into the "lava." To make the game last longer the teams can have to get to the end point and then back to the start. If teams run into each other they cannot go around, they must find another way.

Lacrosse Kick Ball
Skills (moving ground balls, conditioning, teamwork)

Players set up just like regular kickball. Instead of kicking the ball, the ball will be rolled with the stick to the person at bat, that person will pick up the ball and roll it to the outfield and then run the bases. To get a player out the ball must be rolled to the base and scooped up by the person on that base. They get three pitches to try to scoop the ball as it comes towards them, if it goes past them then it's a strike. Rules: no throwing the ball at a person or tagging a person with the ball.

Tunnel Races:
Skills (conditioning, upper body strength, agility, teamwork)

Give everyone a partner (have a group of 3 if odd numbers) Each partner group gets on the end line. The first partner runs out to a spot marked with a cone or use lines on the field and turns sideways to become a bridge. The second partner runs out, crawls through the bridge, runs to the next cone and then becomes a bridge. They alternate being a bridge until getting to the specified end line and then they both must bear crawl together back to the start, sit down and put their hands up signaling that they are done.

Indoor Dog Sled race:

Skills (upper body strength, conditioning, teamwork)

On a gym floor, partner up the players. One player is given a towel to sit on (if no towel it may work to take off shoes and use socks if there is no risk of splinters, etc) The other player holds a rope and gives the other end of the rope to their partner. They must pull their partner to the other side of the gym where they will switch places and then get back to the starting line. This is also fun if you have some old boxes that can be pushed across the floor with a partner inside the box.

Zombie Tag
Skills (Conditioning, competition, agility)

Make a large circle and have all the girls go inside, they must stay inside the boundary. They don't need any equipment, they will all be trying to tag each other when the game starts. When a player is tagged they must leave the circle, run around the outside of it and then they may go back in but they must lose a limb before they can re-enter. The first time they are tagged they will put an arm behind their back. Then the other arm, next a leg, finally both legs are out and they must crawl on their knees. Once they are tagged while on their knees they are officially out of the game. They may tag with any part of their body that is not lost from being tagged. While the players are doing their lap around the circle they can use all of their arms and legs until they re-enter the circle.

Rocking Puppies
Skills (cradling, coordination, stick-work)

Small stuffed puppies can be found at the dollar store in the toy section. Hand those out to players and have them put the puppy inside the pocket of the stick facing out. Have players walk to field while "rocking" their puppy to sleep on their right side and then on their left side. The puppy should face out at the start and face the player at the middle in front of her face before coming back to the shoulder and facing out again. Handle should be at an angle with the bottom hand out away from the body so that the puppy stays safe and snug in the stick.

Coaches
Bag-O-Tricks

Emergency Kit

Inside the Coach's Bag of Tricks:

- A women's lacrosse stick (boys sticks don't throw the same, if you are coaching girls you need girl's equipment)
- An extra stick if you have one, someone always forgets one, breaks one, or needs one for some reason or another
- Extra goggles – same reason and they can't play without them
- Rope – best tool for explaining shooting angles and shooting space
- Clipboard/white board to draw up concepts for visual learners, keep track of names, notes from practice, practice plan, etc
- Different types of lacrosse balls – soft balls for learning in a safe environment, regular lax balls, reaction ball for goalies
- Playground and/or dodge balls for teaching concepts without having to worry about the level of stick skills. Easy to throw and catch.
- Cones: you can run a whole practice with no net or lines as long as you have a good amount of cones in the bag!
- Sunglasses, sunscreen, hat. Summer or winter, protect yourself!
- A fun option for conditioning. Giant foam dice with different activities on each side. Need a fun activity? Let em ROLL THE DICE!
- Whistle
- Stickers make great rewards throughout practice, they can stick em on their forehead, their stick, etc.
- First aid Kit and medical emergency info, parents contact info, extra water
- Grab Bag of dollar store goodies for those days no one is paying attention. Pull that out as the ultimate prize and use it sparingly to keep the excitement up for it when it does come out.

DRILLS

Drills that focus on:

Pivoting, Cutting, and Space Awareness

Pivot and Pick Up Drill

Focus: Pivoting off of correct foot, pushing off after the turn for burst of speed, looking up to find ball right away.

Equipment needed: Cone for each small group, ball for each group (you can use a lacrosse ball but a tennis ball or playground ball will be easier to grab and safer) For advanced players, you can progress to using sticks and ground balls and then passes, and right/left hand, and even catching on the back of the stick, only after the pivoting concept is done correctly.

How it's done: Two partners, one cone about 15 yards out. One partner runs to the cone, plants correct foot and pivots, turns and pushes off. The other partner will roll a ball out as she is running back and she will try to grab the ball on her way to the start line. The partners then change roles.

Set up several groups going all at the same time.

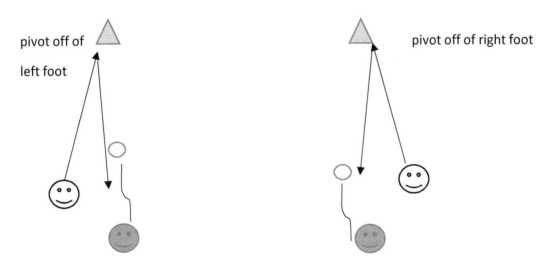

pivot off of
left foot

pivot off of right foot

Cutting Stations

Set up several stations with different kinds of cuts (some examples below), have a short line at each station. Each player performs the cut and then comes back to ask for the ball from the next person in line. After several minutes have each line rotate to a new station.

Focus: using proper footwork and eyes up to find the ball

Equipment needed: playground or other easy to catch ball, more advanced players can progress to using sticks and balls after running through it without sticks. FOOTWORK is most important here.

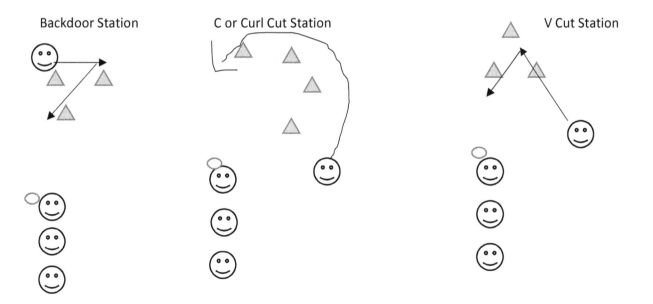

Backdoor Station   C or Curl Cut Station   V Cut Station

Space Camp Tag

Tag game that works on finding open space in a large area as well as man to man marking within defendable length. The idea is to keep offense focused on finding their own space, away from defense and away from their own players. Defense is focusing on keeping themselves within defendable position of someone on the other team who is not already being marked.

Equipment needed: Large area to play tag in, reversible pinnies, whistle

One team is "it" and they are trying to stay within reach of someone on the other team. The team that is not "it" is trying to stay as far away from everyone, including their own teammates, as possible. The whistle will randomly blow (or play music and have the music stop) and everyone MUST freeze. The players who are "it" get one step to try and touch someone on the other team, if they can then that person within reach is out (or can join the "it" team) If any players who are not "it" are within touching distance of someone on their own team they are also out (or joining the "it" team)

Blindfold Cat and Mouse Chase:

Works on Communication, spacing, awareness, following and giving directions.

Put two players inside of a 5 by 5 yard box and cover their eyes with a blindfold or blacked out sunglasses. Each player will have a helper who is directing them. The cat is trying to tag the mouse but neither of them can see each other. The directors must communicate and try to help the mouse get to a safety cone, and help the cat to find the mouse before it finds the cone. The directors must also keep the players in their box area. After they finish the directors and cat and mouse will switch roles. They will learn to give specific directions and see how important communication is.

Stick Work

Everyone Grab a Ball and get ready for stick-work FUN and Challenges!

No matter what you're groups skill level is, every age benefits from starting at the beginning and progressing up. Whether it's from bad habits, or they never got the mechanics right from the start, here's a progression to get them moving their feet, softening their grip, adding wrist flicks and tracking the ball. Grabs some goggles and a mouth guard too!

1. Put the stick in your right hand by your side, grip it about a fist length down from the head. The pocket is facing the sky and the ball is sitting in the pocket. Use the thumb on the top of the stick for control. Lightly use your wrist and a little arm to flick the ball up. Catch it with relaxed arms, bent knees, super soft and get used to the feeling of the give with the ball. Repeat several times and then try again on the other side with the left hand.
    *if needed, the player should move their feet to get to a ball that is tossed too far away rather than reaching with the arms. Get used to moving **to** the ball!*

    PROGRESS IT when they look ready:
    Flip it up and catch it on the back of the stick
    Flip it up and catch it up by the shoulder
    Flip it up, switch hands and catch it by the other shoulder
    Flip it up, catch it by the shoulder on the back of the stick

    Try to flip up two balls at once very lightly and then catch them. Can you try 3?

2. Keeping the ball in the stick is a challenge for many kids. Start off by showing them just how G FORCE works to keep it in there. They are also learning how the ball feels when it's in the pocket.

   Progress it: Start by your side, then progress to over the head, and then for fun have them try to go from standing and cradling in front to kneeling and then to laying on their backs and trying to cradle without dropping the ball.

3. Another way to practice body movement and keeping the ball in the stick is walking alternating leg lunges while feeding the stick through the legs with a ball in the pocket.

   Progress it: You can do this as an activity by itself, but you can also add on and make this something they do 3 times before entering a drill. For example- attack is going to cage, defense must feed the ball through their legs 3 times before they can enter the drill and mark up. The more stick/body/ball awareness they have, the better their stick work will become.

   Progress it more: Try to do this with 2 or 3 balls in the pocket with the goal of not dropping them, make it a race, make it a contest for how many balls they can carry without dropping...

4. Tunnel Pass: the balance between relaxed arms, comfortable but controlled grip, wrist flick and momentum are all practiced in this pass to yourself. Wide squat stance, one hand on the stick, the ball is tossed through the legs and behind you, up in the air and then comes down in front where you attempt to catch it.

    Progress it: Do this pass with a partner, you both pass it through the legs and then up and over to the partner who is across from you, both balls going at the same time and you try to catch your partner's ball.

    Progress it more: Spin around 3 times and then try to pass it to your partner. Seems silly but in a game players find themselves having to quickly recover, find their space and get the ball to a safe location.

SCOOPING
Ground Balls

(Individual)

Drop step stationary ground ball scoop:

For introducing the skill to new players.

Each player gets a ball. Place the ball between the player's legs. They will drop step the left leg and then get low to scoop the ball. Place the ball back and repeat but on the other side with the stick in the left hand. **FOCUS:** top hand high on the stick, bend knees to get low, push through the scoop and bring the stick back up.

Puppy Rescue:

Put dollar store little stuffed puppies out on the field. Line the players up across and end line. On the whistle the players will run out, pick a puppy to scoop and then cradle the puppy to sleep as they continue to the other side of the field.

Rolling ball scoops:

Each player rolls the ball out on their own, then scoops it. Progress it to each player rolling their ball out and then attempting to quickly scoop up someone else's ball before it stops rolling.

Pizza Scoops:

In groups of 3, players form a triangle, each with their own ball. Players will roll the ball to the person to her left, then run and scoop the ball coming at them from their right side. Continue around the triangle several times and then switch direction. For the young kids, let them decide what flavor of pizza their group is running around.

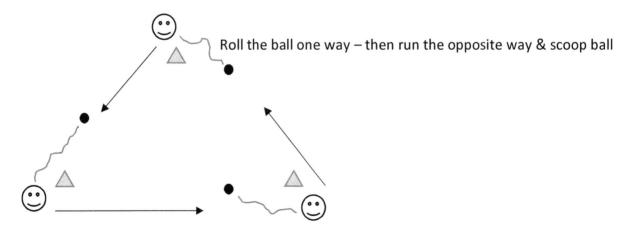

Roll the ball one way – then run the opposite way & scoop ball

Tunnels:

 Start off with pairs, one player uses their stick to make a tunnel and the other player must go under the tunnel to scoop the ball. Have each player take a turn being the tunnel and the scooper. Focus on getting low, top hand up high on the stick, scooping the ball cleanly without pop ups, bringing the stick all the way up, stick protection and getting their eyes up to look for trouble. (focus on one piece of that at at time)

Progress it: Have the tunnel players spread around the field or gym each with a ball under their tunnel. The scoopers will line up at the end line and on the coach's signal they will run out and scoop as many balls as they can in a minute. The player with the most balls wins. Switch the tunnels and scoopers and go again.

Progress it more: Try to have more tunnels than scoopers or to make it more like musical chairs, have less tunnels than scoopers.

AMP up the FUN FACTOR:

Bring your Bluetooth speakers and play music to make play live, freezing when the music stops.

Have the tunnels move to a new spot every few seconds to make it a super challenge!

SUMO – the box out drill:

Line players up back to back on a field or gym line. No sticks, just use hands to start with. Place a ball between them on the line. Their heels must be in front of and on their side of the line that is between them. On the whistle, players will attempt to get low and box out their partner. They cannot just reach down and grab the ball, they must back up and get their entire foot over the line behind them before they can try to pick up the ball. If they fall down they must start again.

Progress it: Add sticks and after the box out they try to scoop the ball with their hands high up on the stick.

Progress it more: After the ball is scooped up the player attempts to get the ball to a cone that has been set out. The other player will immediately play defense and try to keep them from touching the cone.

Make it a group game: Have them work in teams to get the most players scoring points by trying to win the box out, scoop up the ball, and then get it to into their team's goal.

Catching and Throwing

Partner Passing Circuit: A million ways to move the ball

Here's some ideas to get your creativity started....

1. Underhand pass without stick to a partner who has a stick. Aim pass for above the shoulder on their stick side. Focus: Stick up giving passer a target, let the ball push the stick back and drop step the leg on the stick side for a giving motion. Avoid going out to meet the ball or wrap catching. (snatching it out of the air)

2. One handed overhand passing – one hand throws using wrist and arm to get the ball there. Stick should start back over the shoulder, flat like holding a tray and then follow through with the wrist. Pass to a partner who has a stick or throw to open space.

3. Triple threat and protect stick: Two handed passing, upon receiving the ball the player will take a few steps back towards their stick side with their stick back and protected almost like a rope is pulling the stick and leading them back, then step forward and throw.

4. Soft hands catching and throwing: have players use the back of their stick to help promote soft catches and eliminate the wrap motion. Don't forget to try with left and right!

5. Turn your back to your partner and send the ball through the legs

6. Bounce it for a once bouncer pass

7. Have your partner hold their stick out to the side, try to get the ball right into their pocket without them having to move.

8. Try super high passes that you have to jump to catch

9. Throw passes short so your partner has to run in and time catching them

10. Throw intentional bad passes and challenge each other.

Go Fish:

Work on moving your feet, looking up, and while focusing on catching and techniques.

In this drill there will be post players in a line who will throw the ball and then receive the ball back on the ground. The catchers will start in a line, the first player will receive a ball from the first post player and then roll it back to them. They will quickly hustle forward to get a ball from the next post, and then roll it back to them. They continue until they have received a ball from each post player. Once they are complete they will take the place of a post player and the post player will become a receiver. They are catching the fish in the air and then rolling it back (go fish) Add a timer for an extra challenge.

Progress it: For advanced play, add posts on either side so they practice receiving the ball both left and right.

Progress it more: Add in a time factor, have several groups race or race against their own time.

Leading Passes:

Leading pass box: 4 cones, 4 players, two leading passes continuously repeating as players work on timing and receiving without slowing down. The players should be all moving to the next cone with each pass. For new players start with a ground ball to introduce the concept of leading with a pass for the passer, and the concept of moving through getting a ball for the receiver.

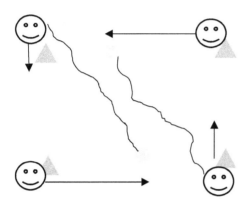

Progress it! Add a defender in the center trying to knock down passes. This makes the feeder have to find passing lanes.

Keep a pile of balls near stations and wait to collect them after the drill. This means less wasted time chasing passes and more time learning and hands on repetitions!

The SNAKE Drill:

Passing on the move, working the ball down the field, transition, pressure all come out of the snake drill. The drill starts with a ground ball scoop and then works from player to player while they work their way down the field. Several balls should be moving down the snake to keep the amount of ball touches as high as possible.

Put out ground balls along the side of the field. The first person will pick up each ball and get it moving down the snake. The second row will join the snake when the ball reaches the 4th player. Follow the squiggly line to see the path of the ball. For young or new players this drill can also be done as a ground ball drill. For advanced players the ball can be caught using left and right hands and you can time the snake to see how long it takes the "tail" (last player) to cross the line.

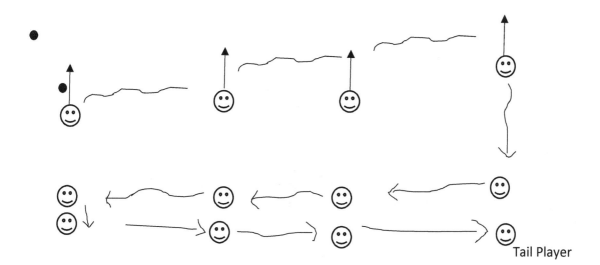

Tail Player

More Leading Passes:

4 Cones around the center circle in the field. A line of players at each cone, and a pile of balls at each cone. The first person will start running to the next cone counter clockwise, as they start moving the person at the next cone also starts to move. Player 1 makes a leading pass to player 2 and then gets at the end of the line at cone 2.

When player 2 recieves the ball, they keep moving and pass a leading pass to player 3 who is now on the move. This is continuous around the circle. The goal is to keep everyone moving around the circle and try to work on getting passes in front of someone rather than behind them. Don't forget to ask for the ball out in front.

Progress it: Rotate to go clockwise instead to work on the left hand passing and catching. Add more balls in, add more lines in, turn it into ground balls instead of passes, put defense(sharks) in the middle of the circle trying to intercept air passes or ground balls coming through.

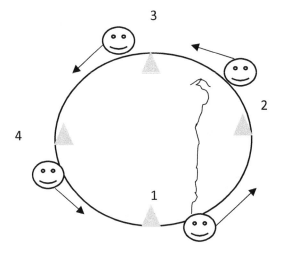

The Hamster Drill:

Two posts, one little cute hamster stuck in the middle going back and forth. The posts each have a ball. Assign one post as the ground ball post and the other as the passing post. The hamster has no ball to start with.

The hamster will run away from the ground ball post, tap the cone with their foot and then pivot, cut back and receive a rolling ground ball. They will scoop the ground ball and then roll it back. After they roll it back they will pivot and cut towards the other post and receive a pass, give it one cradle and then throw it back. They continue going back and forth for a timed period (a minute to 90 seconds is a good amount of time, they should be pretty tired!)

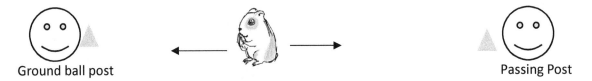

Ground ball post   Passing Post

Competitive Ground Balls

Slumber Party:

Split the group into teams, start with two teams but you have the option to have many teams competing at once – just assign them their own home base. Each team will go to opposite sides of your practice area with their equipment, lay down and pretend to sleep. They will need to assign a lookout person who will keep their eyes up to watch for the ground ball entering the competing area. Use cones or lines to define the in-bounds play area. Once the ball is released, the teams are woken up by their team's lookout person who will shout "MIDNIGHT!"

The players will run into the play area, try to gain possession of the ground ball and get the ball out of the play boundaries and back to their slumber party area. The team with the most balls at the end wins.

Progress it: Require a certain amount of passes before they can take the ball out. Roll more than one ball in at a time.

Ground Ball Numbers Game:

Two teams, one on either side of the coach. The coach has a pile of balls and will roll a ball out one at a time. Coach will announce a number the represents how many players from each team will go out after the ground ball. If the coach says 23, that means 2 from the team on the coach's left side and 3 from the team on the coach's right side. Use any numbers up to 7 v 7.

Progression: have a required number of passes after a team gains possession. Give extra points for clean pick-ups. (no pop ups) Have the teams go to goal. Add additional players in after possession is established to help get the ball to goal and work on transitional concepts.

4v3 and 3v4 Around the Goal:

Moving around in a small space, making quick decisions, grabbing the ball in a scrum and keep it safe, maximizing scoring opportunities and defending a critical situation all get some attention in this box drill around the cage. Add requirements to change the challenge such as number of passes, types of shots allowed (only low or high, from a certain hand, from a certain spot, etc).

Whoever gains possession of the ball is offense, other team becomes defense. Offense goal is to score or hold onto the ball for a certain amount of time, defense is trying to get possession and clear it out of the box or to force a poor shot for a goalie turnover. The coach can roll the ball in from various sides of the box and with no notice so the players must be ready to go and watching for it. The ball entering the box signals the start of the drill.

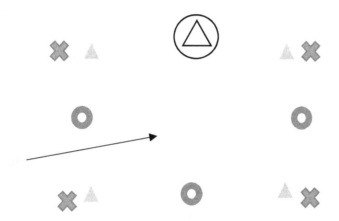

GB Battle:

The ball is rolled into the middle of the 8 in front of the goal. Players from both teams have their back to the ball, facing the sidelines. On the coaches signal play becomes live and the assigned defense team will try to clear the ball out as quickly as possible or get it to the goalie. Attack will try to gain possession and score or pull the ball out of the dangerous area in front of the goal to start a slow offense. You could have the offense bring the ball out wide and have to complete a full cycle of passes around the 8 meter area without turning it over.

Royal Family (queen) of the hill Ground balls:

Just like it sounds, the battle is to keep your team on top of the winning hill. Each win sends you toward the top and each lost sends you back down. Teams can be any size up to 7, but I prefer smaller groups like 2 or 3. All the teams must be the same size or very close to the same size. For small groups you can do 1v1 instead of teams at each station. *With a 1v1 situation, give them 3 tries to win the ball at each station. The player that gains possession the most times out of 3 moves up.*

Separate the field into different stations of ground ball competition areas. One station is the top of the hill and then figure out which way leads down to the very bottom of the hill. At each station have a pile of balls and if possible separate the teams so they wear the same color, they can switch pinnies around at each station if they need too.

Roll the ball out, both teams at that station race to get possession of the ground ball and keep possession for a full minute. The catch: they can't hold the ball for more than 4 seconds after they gain possession. The team with possession at the end of the minute moves up the hill, the team that losses possession starts going down the hill. IF the winner is aleady at the top, they stay. If the loser is already at the bottom then they stay.

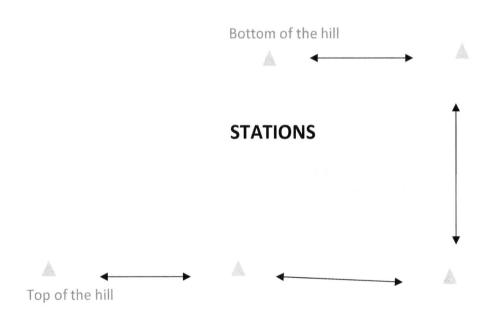

49

Building an OFFENSE

Changing direction:

Using cones in a zig-zag patterns, players practice changing direction while keeping possession of the ball and protecting their stick. At each cone the player will plant, push off to the new direction, and switch hands with their stick. This can be set up all over the field or with a goal at the end of it and a shot.

Progress it: time it or have several groups racing each other, starting over anytime the ball is dropped. Put the zig zag of cones in front of another drill where the players must go through the cones before being able to run into the drill.

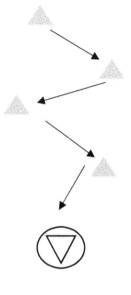

Use the zig-zag drill without sticks. Have the players go quickly through tagging each cone with a hand for agility, quickness and cardio conditioning.

Dodge and tag:

Dodging can feel complicated to youth players. I prefer to look at dodging as just getting around something to avoid a collision and keep from losing the ball. High Fives and a blow up Hulk can do the trick just fine! Work on footwork before adding sticks and stick protection. Three helpers stand in a triangle ready to high five the players. A player runs and plants a foot left, high fiving the person on their left, then they take a giant leap to high five the person on their right, the step to box out the HULK (or chair or whatever you have handy) and high five the last helper and then continue to receive a playground ball tossed to them and then then throw it into the goal (or bucket, or whatever you have)

Progress it: take away the high five helpers and put cones in their place. Have them dodge using the cones. Then add sticks and stick protection.

Hunger Games: (learning a settled offense, the fun way)

Start with no sticks, use an easy to throw around playground ball. Put out 7 markers around the goal (I used different colored Frisbee golf discs from the dollar store but cones work too) Put a player on each spot and one in the goal (8 players total). They don't need any goalie stuff or gear because you are not using a hard ball ball. Adjust number of spots to the amount of players you have participating to more or less.

How you play the game: Players may only stay on their spot for 3 seconds max, they must get off of their spot before the end of 3 seconds and find a vacant spot to move to. There can only be one person on each spot at a time.

One player starts with the ball. While players are changing places they may also try to run through the cornucopia area in the center, where they can receive a pass and shoot. Like the other spots, they may only be in the cornucopia for 3 seconds at a time. You can start with a 3 pass rule before they can try to shoot if they are shooting too soon.

After every round, let a new player try to be in the goal. Have the goalie communicate where the balls is and direct players to open spots.

The ball can be passed to a player who is on a spot around the outside, or to a player in the cornucopia area, you cannon run around with the ball.

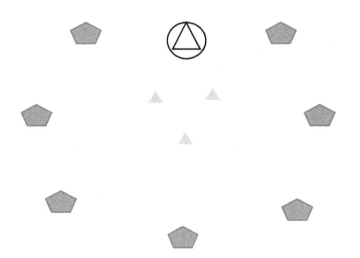

Progress it: Add Defense, The goal of defense is to get possession of the ball. They can also tag a player who is on a spot more than 3 seconds and then they get to switch places with them as offense/defense.

Blow a whistle at random times that signals them to freeze to try to catch players who are not on a spot so that they move quickly from place to place.

Battle Slugs:

Work on cutting to get open, finding passing lanes and quick thinking. You can start this with a tennis balls to throw by hand and no sticks and then progress from there to sticks and lacrosse balls.

The balls start at one end. The X team is trying to get the balls from person to person all the way to their home base. The O team is trying to steal possession of the balls and get the balls back to the start. Players can move around in their area by their cone but no further than that. They must throw to the player next to them, no skip passes. The first X player picks up a ball and then play is live.

Let X and O switch roles after each round. The drill goes by time, for example 3 minutes to try to get all the balls to the other side, one point for each ball they successfully get there by the whistle, and one point for the other team or all the balls they keep the team from getting there.

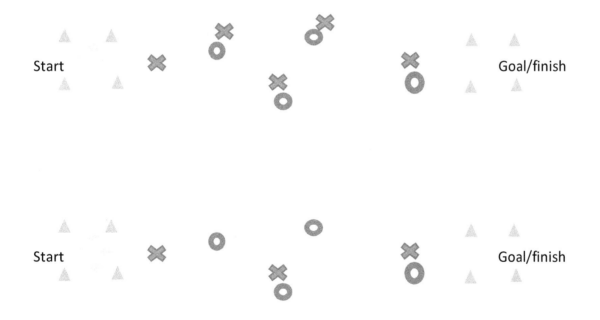

Cut and Tag:

 Getting the concept of movement can be tough for kids. Add in tag and make it a snap! Set the girls up on the 7 spots and give the ball to a player down by the goal. The person on the other side of the goal will go first. Tell them a number from 1 to 5, that number is how many tags there must be before the person with the ball will pass it to someone to score.

If you say 3, the first person will choose anyone they want to run to and high five them and take their spot. The person they tagged will run to another spot and high five someone and take their spot. The third person gets to run towards the goal to receive a pass and shoot. It helps to have them count out loud as they do each high five so they know what number they are on. They will cut one at a time and only if someone comes to high five them. Let different people take turns being the person to have the ball, different people to start, and vary the number of cuts each time. To progress it, give them sticks and a ball and eliminate the high five.

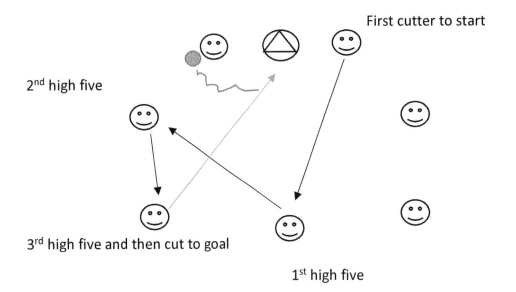

First cutter to start

2nd high five

3rd high five and then cut to goal

1st high five

Give and HEY!!!!! Give it back!! (give and go)

Great concept for kids to learn, get comfortable with and master. The give and go. This is a line of give and go action where after they give and then get the ball back, they pass it up to another person to do the same thing. Then the ball comes back the other way, repeat several times and don't forget to have them switch places with the post passers.

Set them up with cones as a guide, player with the ball passes it to the post, then sprints to the next cone where they will get the ball back and then pass it to the next player who will do a give and go. Start with a kick ball or dodge ball to throw before trying to do this with sticks and a ball.

Progress to balls and sticks, left hand going one way and right hand on the way back. You can have several lines of these going at once.

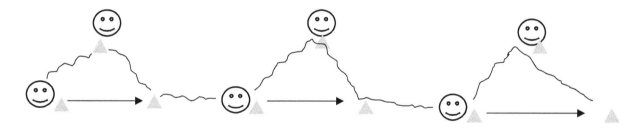

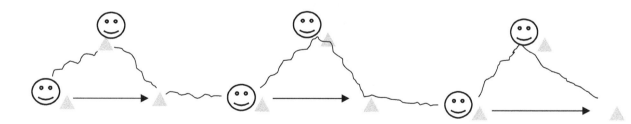

The Shooting Station:

Break down shooting to footwork first, then sticks. The added bonus of this is allowing anyone to try the goalie experience because you are shooting with kick balls, dodge balls or even stuffed animals.

Put out as many goals as you can drag around, 3 or 4 is a great number but 2 works also. Each goal is a station and should have a different kind of shot. My favorites to start with are crease roll, a feed and a shot, and an 8 meter. The goal here is repetition so avoid over coaching the shooting and let them work it out by doing it as much as possible and keep the lines short. After a certain amount of time, signal for the groups to rotate stations and goalies.

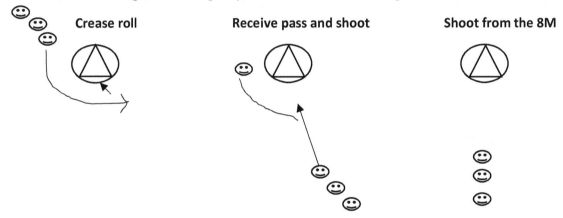

At the crease roll station: Put a cone out in front of the goal to show where the players need get too before shooting for the best angle.

Always put out crease markers so they get used to working around it.

Encourage running through the shot so they don't stop their feet. At the feed and shoot station encourage trying to throw in a simple fake before shooting (for example, all shots will be fake left high, then shoot right low)

Shooting Aids:

Make shooting FUN! From clinics and coaches all over the country, these are my favorite shooting ideas for practice!

Cheap grocery or dollar store metal cake pans! Drill two holes in the top and use string to tie them up anywhere in the goal or in the upper corners. Award points for the loudest clang shot into the pans.

Bungee Wedding Dress Goalie: Grab an old dress out of the closet or from a thrift store, the fancier and more ridiculous the better! Use bungee cords through the arm holes to hang it in the goal as your goalie.

The obstacle course: drag anything you can get your hands on out onto the field, or have players make agility poles by standing in place, or making a bridge on their hands and feet. The players must hurry through the obstacle course and get their shot off before time runs out.

Horse for Lacrosse: Make a shot, any shot you want, and the players behind you must make the same shot or get a letter until they spell horse.

Around the world for lacrosse: Set up your 9 spots and the order, players try to get around the world and back. They can chance a missed shot and risk starting over – same as basketball.

Over the Top: Place a goal behind another goal just a few feet. The players will try to shoot over the top of the first goal and into the goal behind it. Side arm shots get no points. Helps with reinforcing the up/down over the top motion.

Basic and Easy offense movement for middle school players:

Sometimes it's difficult getting the offense to move. Once they know the settled offense spaces to get too, they need a pattern to get them moving. The pattern may fall apart, but in the end, if they move – something happens and that's the goal.

Here the home base is the top left corner, that's where the ball starts and where the ball heads back to if no shot is available. The ball is passed to the top middle player who will drive in to goal. If they don't have the opportunity to score then they will pull out and take the spot of the person that threw the ball at home base. While that player is driving the rest of the offense is shifting counter clockwise one spot and the process starts over again. While players are shifting they should also see the ball and be ready to grab a loose ball if it's dropped or rebounds from a shot.

Progress it: Pass the ball twice, every one bumps over two places, ball still settles back at home base at top of left corner if no scoring opportunity is available. Progress it again by passing it 3 times and bumping 3 places around the clock pattern. Do they have this down? Try it in reverse, pass it the opposite way and bump clockwise.

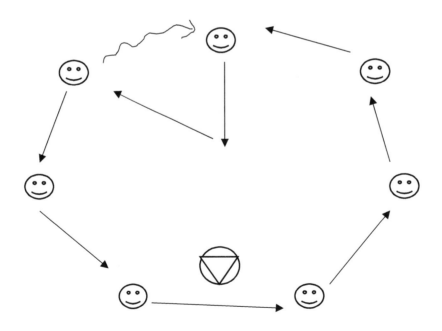

Down the ocean, hon!

Or down the field at least....

Midfield Transition

Mooove that ball: The great COW Race

Make teams of 4 or 5 players each and put them on the end-line. Each team has a pile of 3 balls at their home base. On the whistle, the teams will work together to get the first ball down to their team's bucket at the other end. They are working the concept of passing and the moving ahead to keep progressing the ball forward.

The players may not take more than 3 steps when they have the ball.

The players may roll or pass the ball to a teammate, but each teammate on the team must touch the ball before any of the teammates touch it again. (Ensures that all players get ball touches)

The players should try to spread out to have options on every side of the ball carrier and not be close enough to touch each other.

Once they get the ball to the end and in the bucket, the whole team must run back to the start and repeat the process until all 3 balls are in the bucket. They are finished when they get back to the start line and act like cows (moos and all!) to signal they completed the task. Assign a winner of the race and also a winner of the best cows ☺

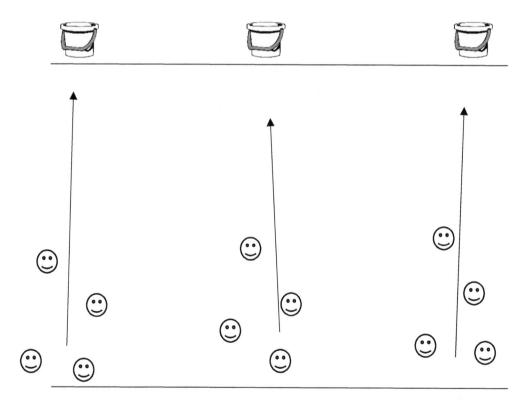

Roll the Dice!

Line em up, have the first person roll the dice and that's how many people on their team will be bringing the ball up the field. Not only does it tell them how many but also what shape. If they roll a 5 then 5 players will bring the ball up the field and they need to keep the shape of the dots on the dice as they move up the field. They also have to make double their number in passes to get there. If they roll a 5 then they must complete a minimum of 10 passes before getting to the end of the field. Each player must touch the ball twice.

Several teams can be going at once, as long as there is enough space for them to spread out and pass to each other. You can have the team waiting behind them start after the first team gets halfway down the field. If they roll a 1 then they toss it to themselves and head down the field.

Below the team on the left rolled a 5 and the team on the right rolled a 6.

Transition to Scoring Area:

As the ball moves down the field, attack and defense need to find the best place to go, mark up, find space, leave a lane to goal, get someone behind the goal and more. So many things to think about, it makes sense to get lots of practice figuring it out.

Start 3 midfielders above the restraining line. Put three defending midfielder with them marked up just behind them so they have to catch up. Pair up 4 attack/defense players and put them out wide in the attack zone. Roll the ball to a midfielder, this starts the drill. As the midfielder brings the ball down, the attack and defense pairs will come in to play and they will need to stop the fast break, cover the dangerous players and start communicating. This drill will often look messy as they trial and error different attempts. To get them thinking, ask them after each round who the most important players are, how they think they can stop the fast break, which players they may be able to leave to help some double team. Etc. Ask the attackers where they could go to be the most helpful and open.

It's easy to get caught talking through this drill too much and giving too many directions. Focus on one piece at a time and learning through doing. This drill is also great for conditioning!

Buzz words I like to use for defense are: tagging in (get to the 12 meter and pick up players in the middle first, like they are tagging someone in the middle), Calling out (announcing what player you have, announcing what players you see that still need to be marked), Sticks in (putting sticks toward the middle to cut down on passing and shooting lanes and Ice Cream cone (staying out of the imaginary ice cream cone that comes from the girl with the ball, AKA shooting space).

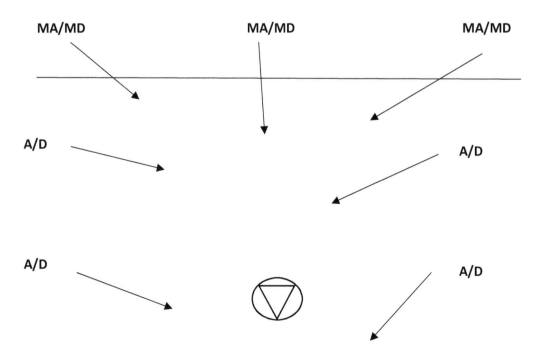

Defense Rocks!

Mirror Mirror on the wall...who's the best defender of them all?

The best piece of defense I learned was how to mirror. Mirror my stick with the stick of the person I'm guarding, mirror my steps with theirs, and then getting to the point where I could anticipate their next move. This is a skill that can be worked on and mastered for years.

Pair the players up, one with a ball as the attacker, one without a ball as the defender, standing stationary. They will face each other about a stick length apart. The attacker will cradle the ball and no matter where the cradle it (left, right, high, low), the defender will mirror across from them.

TIP: the ball comes UP when it is thrown out of the stick, it's not released straight, so the defender should mirror the head of their stick slightly ABOVE the stick of the attacker for a better chance of knocking down the pass.

The Moving Mirror:

The next progression of this drill is where the players get a little more freedom to move around. The attacker will keep facing forward but may move and shuffle side to side or back and forth. The defender is tracking the attacker now with their feet and their sticks trying to be the perfect mirror image of them.

The Mirror Box:

Make a box with cones and place an attacker at each cone. The attackers will be throwing around the outside of the box to each other. Place a defender at each cone also, they will be mirroring their attacker in order to deny the pass or attempt to knock down the pass if their player has the ball. Once they get the idea, let the attackers pass in any direction and even across the box.

Knock downs, forcing a bad pass, denying a pass should all be celebrated as much if not MORE than goals scored. Defenders need reasons to feel the importance of their contribution to the team.

Hold the Line

Anticipation is so important in defenders and something we can have them practice from the very start. Line up cones about 3-5 yards apart. Put a pair of players between each set of cones. The attacker will be attempting to get over the line, the defense will work on shuffling back and forth to beat the defender to their attempted path.

Start this drills with no sticks, footwork must be learned first and stick protection makes it too complicated. Work on staying low and quick shuffling. This drill is a great way to let offense practice dodging and cutting as well. If the attacker gets over the line they reset and go again until you tell them it's time to switch roles.

When they are ready to try, add sticks and a ball. Defenders will need to use proper body contact, and attackers will need to keep their stick protected to avoid charging through with the stick.

Red Rover Red Rover, send that attacker over!!

One of my favorite games as a kid (except when you get clotheslined). This safer and lax double team adapted version will likely be a big hit with your players this season.

Line the defenders up, each at a cone about 2 yards apart. Then line up attack across from them about 5 yards out. Assign each attack player a number. The coach will call out a number and that player is attempting to get through the line of defense to the other side (no sticks) The defenders may not use their arms or hands, they must shuffle their feet and try to get their hips together to close the gap before the attacker can get through. You can have defenders put their arms crossed in front of them or hold them behind their back, this is a feet only drill and we don't want any elbows sticking out to impale anyone like poor Olaf.

If the player doesn't get through then they join the defense line. If they do get through then they go back in line with the attackers and keep playing.

Have a large group? Have several of these going at the same time.

Progress it: Allow the attackers to go through any part of the line rather than having to go straight ahead.

Progress it more: Call out several numbers to go at the same time.

Team Defense: I MOVE = WE MOVE

Getting the WE concept of team defense can be a challenge. I use the analogy of a rubber band defensive unit. All of the defenders hips are connected around a big rubber band. The band is tightest near the ball so it pulls harder towards the ball side, it's loosest the farthest away from the ball so it doesn't pull so much over there.

When one defender moves, it pulls all the defenders around them in one direction or another, which means: If one of us moves, WE ALL ADJUST AND MOVE TOO!

Depending on where the ball is, each defender has a different job. Because of this, every single time the ball changes hands, we have to communicate our new job – kind of like instragram!

Im ON BALL

Im HELP LEFT

Im SLIDE or as I like to call it PUSH (because I push the person next to me to go get in the double team while I come take her girl)

Put the players in a big circle of 7 girls. Attackers on the outside and defenders inside facing the person they are marking. Introduce this concept and practice it with a playground ball that is easy to pass around.

Give the ball to an attacker. The ball can be passed either left or right, but cannot be passed until all of the defenders communicate their role out loud. Each time the ball moves, the defenders yell out their new role.

Once they have a good handle on this, start letting the attackers pass the ball using skip passes or across the circle. The defense allows the passes to be made, concentrating on their role and communicating.

Progress it: The attackers may take two steps in, defenders will form double teams to deny them from entering the circle. This will cause the rest of the defense to shift towards the ball, leaving one person open opposite the ball side or two people being marked by one defender.

Progress it More: Put a cone in the middle of the circle, the attackers are trying to get the ball into the circle and tag the cone. Only one person can try to get inside the circle at a time. The attackers continue passing the ball and trying to cut individually into the middle while the defense communicates, slides and double teams.

Progress it MORE: Put the players around the 12, the defenders around the 8 and try the game using the lines on the field. Eventually let them try with sticks but if it falls apart, go back to the playground ball and focus on communication and footwork. Avoid letting the offense make more than one cut at a time as it gets confusing fast.

 Attacker Defender

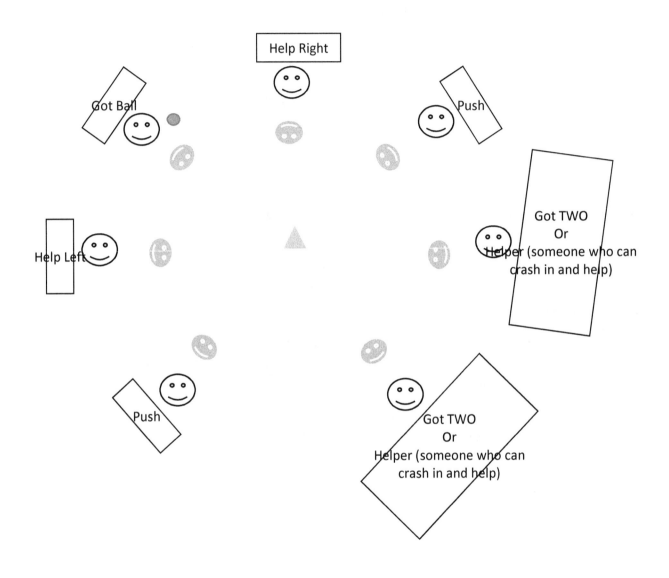

What do I do with my Goalie?

Goalie Wars:

ROUND ONE: Pick two players interested in trying goalie, if no one is interested, they probably will be after you explain this fun activity! Grab a bag of soft toys – you can stock up at the dollar store, garage sales, etc.

Face two goals towards each other about 5 yards apart. Give each goalie the same number of soft toys. If you have an old apron they can stuff the pockets of their apron with the toys, if not they can put them on the ground and grab them from there.

On the start signal the goalies with try to score on each other while also trying to stop the toys from going in their own goal. At the end of the round the goalie with the least amount of toys in the goal gets the point. Have them play several rounds. For more fun let the winner stay and have someone else take the loser's place to rotate more people in to try it.

ROUND TWO: Put out two cones about 5 yards or less apart for each goalie symbolizing a goal line. Goalies will face each other about 10 yards away from each other standing just in front of their own goal line. Goalies will take turns trying to roll tennis balls as fast as they can into the other goalies goal. Have extra balls nearby so they don't spend any time chasing them. Goalies can wear goggles for this in case a ball pops up. If you progress to lacrosse balls put them in full gear. You can even eventually add sticks.

The purpose of this is quick reaction and goalies should attempt to get their body in front of the ball rather than reaching. Quick feet and fast hands are all a part of this fun game. Assign points- first one to 10 wins and then move them to the next Goalie War activity!

ROUND THREE: One goalie lays down by a cone. The other goalie stands about 10 yards away, and throws a bounce pass at a cone that is 5 yards in front of the laying down player. As soon as the laying down goalie sees the ball is being thrown they get up as quickly as possible and try to catch the ball after the bounce. They get a point for a every ball they successfully collect before it bounces twice. They get 10 tries and then switch roles. Use tennis balls, then progress to lax balls with full gear.

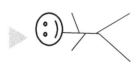

So. Many. Lines. What is the 8 for anyways?

Teach the lines on the field, it's as easy as a story about a trip to Goalie Island. Take your team inside the goal circle, which is also known now as Goalie Island. Enjoy your time there, because after this visit, only the goalie can come inside. You can't even poke your stick into the cool tropical breeze of Goalie Island, not if you're on defense, not if your team has the ball, not even if you're shooting, so soak it all up! If you like Goalie Island an awful lot, think about becoming the goalie!

In front of goalie island is where the shark bait area can be found. The 8 meter is not only 8 meters out from Goalie Island, but it is also where it is rumored that the sharks ATE the shark bait. **The sharks ate the bait inside the 8... true story!**

How do you avoid being shark bait inside the 8 so you don't get.. umm..well.. ate?

The secret is this:

If your team has the ball (attack) you can avoid being seen by the sharks, you can be invisible to them, as long as you keep moving through the shark tank. If you stand still, then beware, sharks can see you standing there!

And defender, if your team doesn't have the ball, you can avoid the sharks too! (to avoid becoming shark bait stew!!) If you are close enough to touch a player on the other team, then you're invisible to those sharks beady eyes, but wander off on your own and you become shark surprise! 3 seconds is all the time you get, to find another person to mark up on or you'll be......
in violation of rule 33 section 10 line 14, heretofore known as the 3 second violation.

Now look ahead, that big line out there. Not that one. The other one. Wayyyyy down the field by the other shark tank. That's the point of no return. Up to 7 people can safely go over that line but 4 friends must remain back along with the goalie. Count out loud as the players cross over – the 4 closest people to goalie island (usually the defenders) will stay behind calling out- 1 2 3 4, everyone else can cross the line.

Copy these and cut them out, have them mark their names on the back and then turn them in for prizes, the chance to lead drills, be a captain, or be assistant coach for a day, etc.

The 4 Cone

Practice Rescue Plan

For Youth Girls' Lacrosse Teams

The **4 CONE** Practice Rescue Plan

No nets, no lines on the field, maybe stuck inside a gym? If you have cones (or anything in your car that you can use for cones) and some balls then you've now got a plan for a practice that's been rescued just in time!

Grab your stack of cones and split it into groups of 4. Each set of 4 will serve as a station so that you can break the kids up into smaller groups for more engagement in each drill. But before you start on drills, don't forget…………….

The Warm UP

Hop on board the **Dynamic Train**! Line 'em up and start moving along the field or around the gym like a giant train, or make several train lines if you have a large group. Every 5 to 10 seconds switch to the next dynamic movement.

1. Walk on toes
2. Walk on heels
3. Pull your knees up to your chest, alternating legs
4. Bend your knee, pull back on your ankle to put heels to rear end, alt legs
5. Walking lunges, alternate legs
6. Walking side lunges alternating sides
7. Hamstring stretch (take a big step with heel on the ground, reach forward and touch toes and then back up again, alternate legs)
8. Jogging high knees
9. Jogging butt-kicks
10. Sideways karaoke-grape vine
11. Sideways karaoke-grape vine facing the other way
12. Squat jumps forward (froggy jumps)
13. Slow jog with large arm swings
14. Medium jog pumping arms ar 45 degree angle
15. Turn and back pedal
16. Done! CHOOOCHOOOOOOOOOO

Get Moving – Inside Out Box Game

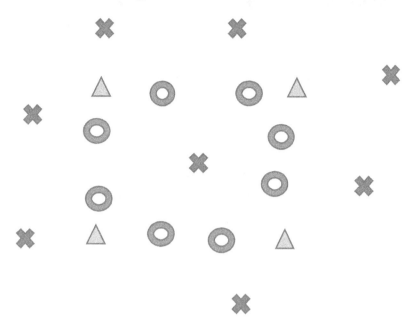

X team has the ball, (for the most fun and involvement, have several balls going at once) on the outside of the cone square. They have one representative who is allowed to be inside the square and can move around anywhere inside. (You can choose to have more than one representative inside) The X team can trade out who is in the middle at any time to get a break, but they cannot carry the ball inside the box.

The O team is around the border of the square protecting the perimeter, they must stay within the square with at least one foot grounding them inside the border. They cannot group around or guard the person in the middle. Just like inside the 8, they can crash in but can't hang out in the middle for more than 3 seconds, except for one O player that may choose to mark up on the inside X.

The object: The offense (X) is trying to get the ball to their inside box representative without it being intercepted by the other team.

Every time the **inside** X gets possession of the ball they get a point. They must then get the ball back outside to their outside teammates and keep trying for points.

If O team gets possession of the ball they switch places and O become the offense team. Count up points for a fun competition.

Use a playground ball or tennis ball or even a shirt tied in a knot. Advanced players can progress to using sticks and lacrosse balls after they have mastered the concept of the game and using body positioning and communication to keep or gain possession. Adding sticks into this too soon, even for seasoned players may decrease the learning of the important positional and problem solving concepts.

BONUS FUN: If you have your coach emergency kit handy, then each point is a sticker

Cat & Mouse

Groups of 3: One Cat, One Mouse, One Grandma

Each group needs their own 4 cone box, to save on cones have adjacent boxes share a wall.

Here's how the story goes. That naughty mouse stole the cat's yummy cheese, and the hungry cat wants it back. Old granny won't have any of this fighting going on in her kitchen! So she puts herself between the cat and mouse to defend her cute little squeakers from that bad old pussy cat!!

If the cat is able to tag the mouse, despite granny's defensive tactics, then the 3 switch roles and try again. Granny should keep her arms crossed out in front of her and the mouse must stay inside the box while trying to keep away from the cat.

This drill works on the cat's ability to dodge, move quickly, be tricky, and beat grandma's defense. Grandma works on her ability to stay between the cat and the mouse, read the cats movements and anticipation. The mouse is working on evading, moving quickly, and working together with grandma to stay safe.

ZIP ZIP ZIPPER Drill

Getting out of trouble when faced with a double team or a crash situation is the ZIPPER DRILL. Pivoting off of the correct foot, keeping eyes facing forward while running out on an angle, with the stick protected are all skills that can be worked on in this cone drill!

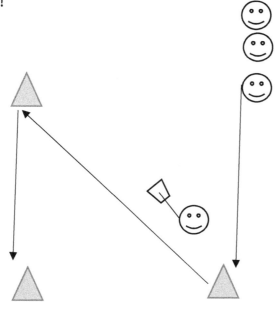

First player will run straight ahead to the first cone where there waits a stationary (or imaginary) double team. The player should break down their steps to slow down and change direction before getting too close to the cones/double team players. They then turn their feet to run out on an angle while keeping their eyes forward. If you add sticks, have the stick back like its being pulled towards the back cone. Once they are at the back cone they will pivot hard and tight and re drive forward to the final cone at top speed. You can add in a pass to another player once they get near the last cone to simulate a shot being taken. Try to start this drill with no balls, just focus on footwork, (turning a tight corner, etc) looking forward, protecting the back shoulder on the back out and good changes of speed. Progress all the way up to adding an actual double team waiting at the first cone.

Conditioning

4 Cones are all you need for a great workout! Make your box anywhere from 10 yards to 20 yards depending on the space you have. Each side of the box represents an activity on round 1. On round 2, each Cone represents an activity. Get creative and change up the activities. Other options include squat jumps, skipping, karaoke, crab walk, hopping on one foot...etc. Repeat rounds but leave adequate time for breaks and recovery. Conditioning is much more fun to music if you have Bluetooth speakers laying around. Play something fast paced and have them try to keep up with the beat.

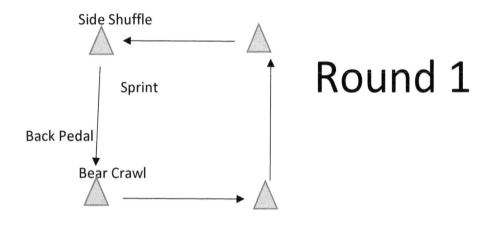

Round 1

Round 2

Run to each station, perform the exercise

And the move onto the next station.

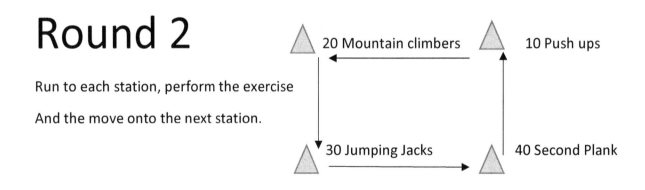

CRASH  DRILL

How do we stop that shooter who is driving to goal? The defensive crash will slow them down and hopefully get them running right back outta there! You can work on the crash without a goal in sight, all you need are those 4 miraculous cones!

The attacker with the ball is trying to get through the box and then pass the ball to their partner on the other side. The 4 defenders, each marking an imaginary attacker at their cone, must communicate the crash, then slide in and try to get that attacker to run back out the top of the box and keep them from getting a good pass off. This drill is more effective if you teach it without sticks first and use a ball they can throw with their hands and then progress. The attacker, if crashed effectively, can practice the back-out skills they just learned in the Zipper.

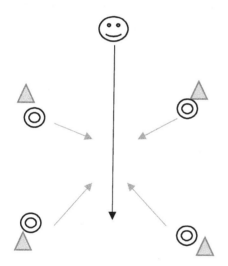

Roll and Cut

Building the habit of passing and then immediately cutting is a skill that these players will use for years to come. In this box drill, players can roll or throw a playground ball, or use sticks and lacrosse balls once they have the concept down. Have as many boxes as you can to eliminate waiting, and this becomes a conditioning drill as well!

Player 1 rolls the ball ahead to the next player (or throws it), then immediately cuts the opposite direction to the open cone. The next player continues working the ball around and cutting to the newly open cone where player 1 used to be. For fun, occasionally make the players switch directions, add in defense at each cone or time them to see which group can get the ball around the most times in a minute.

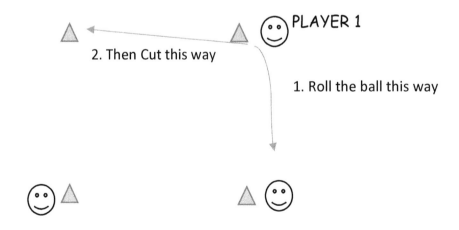

The STICK Game

With a grand total of 0 cones needed for this drill, perhaps it's the most miraculously fun way of all to end your practice! Gather all of your players into a circle, they will need their sticks and nothing else. The sticks will be help upside down with the head on the ground and two fingers lightly holding the top end of the stick. The players will be rotating either left or right on your command.

Practice left and right...and do lots of practice rounds. When you shout LEFT- all of the players will let go of their stick and move left to grab the stick to the left of them. If the stick they are reaching for drops to the ground before they are able to grab it then they are out. If you shout right- then they move to the right. After the eliminated players leave the circle, the remaining players will need to move around to fill in the gaps before going again.

Once there are few players left or no one is dropping sticks, make the players take a step back to make the game harder. Keep going until 3 players are left. Those players will go back to back until you are down to the final winner.

Don't FORGET:

- Even if you are inside, or outside and it's cold out, frequent water breaks are very important for kids who dehydrate very quickly!
- Keep the drill length between 10-15 minutes after you explain and set it up. It always feels longer to the participants than the coach. Time it!
- Also check your watch when you start explaining a skill or drill. Keep it under a minute, make it a game, time yourself and set and alarm, the kids will love when you blow it and get cut off by the bell.
- Allow them to make mistakes a few times before intervening, sometimes they are just working out how to do it in their mind and need a few chances to trial and error a new situation.
- Most importantly, have fun! If they love the learning they will be more engaged and try harder so they can keep doing it!
- Adjust drill sizes and variations to your group of girls based on their abilities, skill level, and how many you have to work with
- Minimize standing and waiting to a point of extinction. Everyone needs a task to do. More than 3 waiting means you have enough to make another station.
- The sillier the reference and analogy, the more fun and memorable it becomes
- Sometimes small spaces and impromptu practices without goals or lines can be the best memories you will have, enjoy a break from the usual grind and celebrate a fun change of pace while still learning to the **Max!!**

Planning for Practice

The most important parts of youth practice are the ball touches and skill repetitions. Design your practice to include as much interaction with the ball as possible for each player. They are building muscle memory, learning how to react to new situations and problems solving skills that will help them grow for years to come.

Less talking, More action = Fast Learning Curve for your team. Youth players learn better by doing, trying, adjusting, rather than by explanation.

Practice SAMPLE:

Arrival Activity: What can players do while other players are arriving? Practicing and/or making up a stick trick, passing with a friend, playing wall ball, or helping drag goals and **10-15 minutes Stick Work Drill:** Individual stick-work led by a coach or high school helper. Pick several variations to work on each practice. Allow them to try it with both hands and progress the skills as they are ready. Focus on effort and helping technique but avoid over coaching as they need reps here and not talking. Add in partner pass if you like here, but passing can easily be incorporated into drills.

5 minutes Dynamic Warm-up

3 Minute Water Break

10 minutes Small Sided Drill (think max ball touches or repetitions and zero line) Groups of 3 -4 players. Triangles, pivot drills, 3 man weave, leading passes, ground all tunnels, cutting drill, etc)

10-15 minutes: Conditioning Drill + water break (make it fun! Could even be tag, it doesn't have to be traditional conditioning …movement = cardio)

5 Minutes Intro Skill of the day: Intro it or review it via demonstration, using buzz words that you can repeat throughout practice, and letting them show you how they do it. **5-10 minutes Progress the skill to 1v1** – slow motion then speed it up, then add a time crunch or repetition goal. Add as many 1v1 stations as possible or pair them up. Groups of 3 you can have one player as the coach/ball roller. By allowing a player to coach they can learn by teaching. **5-10 minutes Progress the skill to add more competitors and a random factor** Throw the ball in from different locations, have varying numbers of players competing, changed number of passes, etc so that they have to think quickly and adjust while practicing the skill

5 Minute Water and Mental Break

20- 25 minutes: Small sided game with emphasis on the skill of the day: 5v5 or less, set up as many stations as you can, think about no standing around or only waiting one rotation. In a pinch a stick work station will keep them busy if necessary. Rotate them quickly in an out and TIME IT. If you have the numbers, work up to 7v7 if they are ready for it.

10 minutes Fun/ team builder/ice breaker activity: not only fun, also add elements of team building, conditioning, movement, and reinforce a love of sports.

Practice Plan

Water Break

Date:_____ Individual Skill Focus: _____

Skills we struggled with last game or practice: _____

Team Concepts needed to work on today: _____

Notes:

Arrival Activity:

Stick Work Drills:

Dynamic Warm up Activity:

Small Skill Drill:

Conditioning:

Skill of the day:

Progressions:

Small Sided Game:

Game/Fun Activity and skill review:

Positions:

4 Defenders: Defense generally starts on the defensive restraining line, marking within a stick length of an offense player. A slower defender may choose to sag back up to 2 stick lengths for a head start, however sagging back more than that typically results in more shooting space violations and the failure to understand how to properly guard a player effectively. It helps to assign a low defender who will be sure that no player from the other team gets behind the defense unmarked. A vocal player is great for this role.

Midfifeld: 3 midfielders, one of which will take the draw, begin the game in the center. One is on the draw line, the other two are outside of the circle. Players outside the circle may move around but may not enter the circle until the whistle is blown. Midfielders cover the entire field and need frequent subbing for recovery. (run 100 yards back and forth for two minutes and you'll get what I mean)

4 Attackers: 4 attack players begin the game behind the attacking restraining line, ready to run in to assist the draw or ready to drop as an option to transition the ball. Attackers generally don't go into the defensive end unless a midfielder is too tired and needs a break. It helps to assign two attackers to take the low spots so that there is always someone behind the goal line extended.

Goalie: put one of your top athletes in the goal, speed, quickness, and great reactive instincts make for a fantastic goalie prospect.

The Draw

The draw can be practiced simply by putting two players together, setting the ball in their sticks and blowing a whistle. This is a great way to get practice taking the very act that helps gain possession at the start of the game.

But there's more to it than that so add in a little extra on footwork and body position.

The BOX out Game for Center Midfielders:
Place two players facing each other on either side of a line as though they are doing a draw, but with no sticks. A third person will toss a tennis ball up in the air between them. The two players must turn their back to box out the other player and then catch the ball in front of them. If they don't have their back to the other player when they catch it then they get no points.
The players should work on good box out positioning and footwork, as well as catching the ball as high in the air as they can. This takes practice as they figure out timing.

Winning the ball for midfielders on the circle: Set up players into two lines. The first two players will go right next to each other in the same way you would set up a throw. Either roll a ground ball or toss up a high ball so players can practice getting the first step, boxing out and reaching and timing to win the ball. The player that wins the ball can throw it back to you, learning to find a passing lane to keep possession after grabbing the ball.

The Dueling Centers: Two center players back to back on a line. On the whistle they must each take two steps forward, turn and find the ball that has been tossed in the air and try to win possession. Play it out until one of the players has gained clear possession of the ball or even let the go to goal or start transitioning the ball to waiting 4v4 attackers and defenders around the 12 meter.

Checking

Youth players don't start checking until middle school, but learning checking techniques early means better skills later on. Checking is all about control, here are some drills that require focus, tight movements and proper mechanics. Oh and they're fun too!

The Fruit Ninja: One player kneels on the ground with a pile of balls. The other player stands across from them with their stick. They should have their hands moved higher on the stick for maximum control. Movements should be quick and be down and up like chopping fruit– not a sweeping motion. The kneeling player will toss balls up to about waist height (away from themselves) and the standing player will "chop" the fruit in half by checking the balls quickly straight down to the ground. The balls can be done slowly one at a time or quickly, or even several balls at once.

The Figure 8: One player holds their arms out in front of them, palms facing each other and about shoulder width apart. The other player will make small movements to trace a figure 8 around the player's hands, carefully working to make controlled movements up and down. They can also do the shape of an M, and a W.

3 seconds Good Defense: In the youth game, defenders who do a great job with body position are rewards with a 3 second good defense turnover. Attackers need to learn early to change the position of their stick to avoid a turn over. In this drill, partner up the players. One has a ball and is walking in place. The other player hides behind the first player and then randomly jumps out to different sides of the player. The attacker needs to switch hands to keep the ball on the opposite side of the defender. This is a great way to improve peripheral vision and reaction time. The next progression, the player simply reaches a stick to one side or the other. The player has to notice the stick and switch hands accordingly. Step it up so that the player only puts a hand over on one side and see if the attacker notices it. The player with the ball has to keep their head on a swivel and be aware of surroundings. Step it up and let them jog down the field doing the same drill.

Coaching Resources

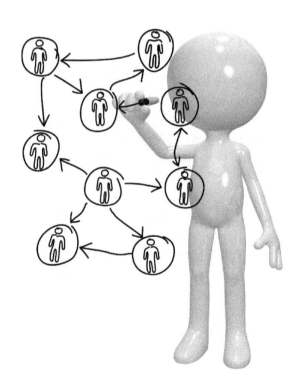

Player, Parent, Coach Expectations

Attendance: Players will notify coaches in the event that they need to miss practice ahead of time except in the case of an emergency.   Attendance is expected at all games and practices, however it is understood that something may come up or an illness may prevent this on occasion. Please keep open communication with your coach via their preferred contact method. Be on time to games, arriving no later than 30 minutes prior to game start time to ensure proper warm up. Traffic is always an issue, please leave extra time for travel. Any player who has had a fever, been vomiting or otherwise too ill to go to school should wait to return to games/practices for at least 24-48 hours after they have time to rehydrate and be prepared to return to vigorous activity.

Behavior: Appropriate language is required at any time on the lacrosse game or practice field or when wearing team apparel, it is important to remember we are representing this team. Respect for our own teammates, our opponents, our opponents fans, our coaches, referees and our opponents coaches is expected at all times. There will be a time that we disagree with one or all of those, and keeping the atmosphere positive will ensure a better experience for our kids and ourselves. Parents are asked to keep cheering from the sidelines focused on praise rather than on directions. Direction coming from both sides of the field create confusion and stress on the players. Coaches reserve the right to ask a player to sit out of a drill if the player is causing disruptive behavior. Our goal is to make this a great learning experience for everyone. Repeated behavior problems will be addressed with a player/parent meeting. If the issues is not resolved, the player may lose the opportunity to play in the next game.

General: Players need to report to games and practice with all of their gear in order to play or practice. This means having their stick – free of broken strings or cracked plastic, mouth guard, water bottle, appropriate shoes, Team pinnie and team shorts once received, and socks on game day. Full uniforms are mandatory both by the league and team for games. Our team has a strict no complaining rule. This goes for coaches, players and parents. The essence of this rule is to keep moving forward through things we may not like, agree with, or that we might find challenging in order to reach for a more important goal in the end. If there is an improvement that could be made, rather than a complaint, we encourage players to self-advocate by approaching coaches after practice with a suggestion for an alternative. Those suggestions will be shared among the coaching staff and admin.

Please give any medical conditions related to your child's participation to your coach in a written note along with an action plan if needed and two contact phone numbers. This includes things such as asthma, heart conditions, learning difficulties, allergies (food, bees, etc)

Player Season Prep Assignment:

Please talk over these questions with your family and fill out on a separate page to bring to practice.

NAME:_____ Team:_____

AGE: _____ GRADE: _____ SCHOOL: _____

1. List some examples of behavior that would make a player look focused and ready to work hard at practice.

2. List some examples of behavior that would make a player look like they were disrespecting their coach and teammates, or being a distraction to those around them.

3. What skills do you think you are best at in lacrosse? What skills do you think need the most improvement?

4. Think of a goal for yourself, something you would like to master before the fall season is over. You can pick up to 3 things, be specific.

5. What are some ideas of ways to get through a situation when you don't like the activity, or maybe find it too challenging, or it's not your favorite thing to do? How can you still do your best when that happens and become a better player? Do you think that could help you in situations outside of sports?

6. If your teammates were to describe you as a person and a player at the end of the season, what do you hope they would say? How do you want to be remembered when this season ends?

7. One a scale of 1-10, 10 being the highest belief and 1 being the lowest belief, how much do you believe that you can master any skill that you put enough effort into this season? Why did you pick that number? What would help you believe in yourself more if it's not a high number?

Parent Questionnaire:

Name: _____ Player's Name:_____

Team:_____ Player's Age: _____

1. What are the 3 top things you hope your child gains from playing this season?

2. What qualities do you find most important when making your choice in a youth athletic program?

3. How does your child learn best?

4. How do you feel about the atmosphere on the parent sideline as well as the appearance of the atmosphere on the coaching/player sidelines? Do you have any suggestions to improve this atmosphere?

5. What does your child enjoy most about playing sports?

6. Is there anything about your child that can help us coach them better?

16 Life Lessons I learned from playing Lacrosse

1. **Life is a series of cuts.** It's all about making choices, changes of speed, and changes of direction. When we stop moving and stand still, our progress stalls and we can't protect the ball.

2. **We need awareness at all times,** to know what the people who are with us are doing, to know what our opponents are doing, and to learn how to work with both of them for the best outcome.

3. **Integrity and sportsmanship** make the game more fun to play, but aren't always easy, especially when the other team doesn't practice them. Keeping those qualities despite what others are doing builds character and feels pretty good at the end of the day.

4. **Anticipating** is always better than reacting.

5. The first one off the line has the opportunity to get the prize, but **the person who is in the best position** usually comes up with it. Attacking goals smarter, not just faster, and with the best effort pays off.

6. **Falling down is inevitable.** Failing to get back up stops the game.

7. Injuries and health problems happen, rest and recovery is essential, but **prevention makes for a much better season/life**.

8. **Mistakes and failures teach us the best lessons**, and those lessons stick with us the longest.

9. **Consistently watching film/reviewing our habits** can show us what we are doing right and where we need to improve.

10. **We don't have to just follow plays,** we can make decisions based on each situation. Adjust on the fly, try something new, never be afraid to drop the ball—it's part of the game.

11. **My role on the team is not the same as everyone else's role,** but I can do my part to the best of my ability and make a difference.

12. **My encouragement and positivity** can change the entire outlook of the team around me.

13. The refs don't always see the fouls that we think we see, but we have to **continue to move forward.** Focusing on the past never changes the call.

14. Sometimes people on the sideline don't know what they are cheering or booing for, so we have to **focus on the task at hand** and let the background noise be just background noise.

15. It may feel like one person is scoring all of the goals, but **the game can't be played alone.** Without the team around them, even the strongest player would have to forfeit.

16. When the season is over, the memories are almost never about the scoreboard, but rather about the **journey and the relationships**.

Side Line Habits of CHAMPIONS

When Champions are on the side-line they:

1. Pay close attention to the game that is playing in front of them
2. Look for players who are playing well and think about how to do the same
3. Look for ways to improve things that are not going well
4. Think of positive things to say to their teammates
5. Cheer loudly and positively in support of the team
6. Are ready to go in at all times
7. Drink some water while waiting to get back in the game
8. Appreciate the hard job of officials and respect their decisions
9. Respect the opportunity to play against opponents and honor the players on the other team with how they act and what they say.
10. Find gratitude in all situations, because they understand that there is always something to be learned, even when it feels difficult. Especially when it feels difficult.

BONUS Material!
Includes Coaches Guide 2.0!

THE Practice PLAN:

Station based training means more action, less down time. It means more learning and trying and less watching. It means more conditioning and moving and less standing. Keep them engaged with a fast tempo practice and time goes fast but not wasted.

Break it down

Here's where the whiteboard comes into play. Each station will be written/drawn up on the whiteboard as A, B, C, D, E. In an hour and a half, your practice will look like this:

Start of Practice: (20 Minutes)

1. Icebreaker Game (the hug game is my favorite, but tag games are great too!)
2. Warm up – Lap and Dynamic and go over board
3. Assign groups (divide any way that works – age, skills or just evenly) Use colored stickers, give each group a different color to stick on their stick, forehead, whatever.

Stations: (50 Minutes)
A. 8 minutes (whistle, 2 minute water break before next whistle to start next station begins)
B. 8 minutes (whistle, 2 minute water break before next whistle to start next station begins)
C. 8 minutes (whistle, 2 minute water break before next whistle to start next station begins)
D. 8 minutes (whistle, 2 minute water break before next whistle to start next station begins)
E. 8 minutes (whistle, 2 minute water break, meet back for wrap up)

You could also eliminate the E session and bring everyone together for a game-like drill to put the knowledge from A through D into practice.

Wrap Up Session: (20 minutes)

1.Share something they learned from each station, something they want to improve on, what their favorite station was.

2. Collect balls and cones and put away

3. End on a fun game

TIP: Have only an hour? Cut it down to 3 stations and only one fun game either at the end or beginning of practice.

TIP 2: Keep stations simple. Walk around and help each one, or ask a few parents to help oversee stations. BE CAREFUL - make parent volunteers understand they are there to guide and answer questions only. They should not repeatedly stop the action at the station for instruction. Your players need to learn by doing, and self-reflection of what did and didn't work.

Basic tips to keep things MOOOOVING

1. Use a timer, keep games and drills just long enough to get the point across, but short enough that they hope you do it again next practice! Transition fast. Time it, let em have that time to do with as they please, they can talk or drink water or whatever - but when time is up they should be racing back as you countdown.

2. Make transitions a competition (Im closing my eyes and counting to 20, everyone has to be on a cone and holding their stick up before I open my eyes, ready GO!) Don't forget the smile ☺

3. Award ridiculous points! 50 thousand bonus points to the person who scoops all their ground balls with their hand at the top of their stick and boxing out. Oh you just lost 1 thousand points for raking the ball because it hurt my eyes to watch it...(don't forget to use your acting skills. Kids rather enjoy the dramatics :P)

4. Require silly punishments. That was definitely an illegal check, you owe me 3 summersaults before you can get back in this drill, or Go sing a random player happy birthday and get back in line, you have 30 seconds GO! :P

5. Buzz Words Get It Done. Don't talk about it and then show it. Just show it and walk them through it. Skip the part where they stand there and listen to you just talk. They aren't listening (even if they're looking at you...)

6. Be energetic, direct with instructions, silly, relax and make jokes, mess up when you demo, laugh when you drop the ball, high five with reckless abandon, get extremely excited when someone tries something and it works, and make a point of choosing the ones that are really trying to learn the ones who get to demo, pick a drill, etc. Make paying attention, being brave to try new things even if they don't succeed, and trying hard the coolest thing they do every day so they can't wait to show you how hard they can work.

7. Bring something different to practices that make it exciting to come. Maybe it's oreos for the oreo challenge, maybe it's a radar gun for shot speed, running parachutes for relay races while cradling to goal, swimming noodles to chase down people on the field and making catching harder, silly hats they can't let fall off while doing a drill...you name it, if it's something different they will be over the moon for practice and they will work harder. (I know fun seems so counterproductive but it's not, it's a learning, effort, and focus catalyst!)

8. Start practice with a fun game. It takes just a few minutes and no one wants to be late if the most fun part is at the beginning. If they know they are only missing the warm up lap they won't care if they're late..

9. End practice with a recap, encouragement, celebrations. NOT. RUNNING.

10. NOT RUNNING! (If you did your practice right they don't need the running at the end, it should have moved so fast from drill to drill with lots of action and no lines that they should be too tired to run anymore)

Fun
&
Mastery

Concepts and Skills

Getting to Know each other:

DO THIS!

THE HUG GAME – Nothing breaks the ice like a hug! Gather your players into a circle on the field or make a box. They must stay inside and move around away from other players until you yell a number. If you yell six, they must find and be in a group of 6 in a big group hug. Anyone who doesn't get into a group of 6 is out and comes over to the cheering section. Have them spread out and jog around again until you call another number until you get down to the final winners.

DO THIS!

The longest pass competition – on piggy back.

Make groups of four. One player will be on the back of another player throwing to their other piggy back partners. The player on top will have a stick and will do the throwing. With every successful catch they move back a step. Repeat the game after you have winners letting new people be on top.

DO THIS!

Practice golf ball ground ball competition. Throw a ton of ping pong balls or plastic practice golf balls out on the field. With a partner, each pair will go hunting for golf balls. One player is blind folded, the other is directing them to balls on the field to scoop up. Once its in their stick and upright they can collect the ball and go find another one. The little plastic balls are hard to feel and harder to scoop up and helps with communication, teamwork, and proper mechanics. Oh yea, and its crazy fun :P

DO THIS!

HOOLA passing competition – Make groups of 3. One person has a hoola hoop and stands between their other two players who will be passing the ball back and forth. They count every time they get it through the hoop and end with a successful catch. The hoop holder can move to increase chance of success. For the teams with the highest numbers, make the hoops have to be stationary and determine if they will be held higher or lower anywhere within the hoop holders reach to make it hard!

NOT THAT!

Let's play the NAME GAME (sit around a circle learning names. SNOOZE!) Or think you skip ice breakers all together… shy players do not play well because they don't want to be embarrassed! The faster they laugh and feel ok to be themselves the sooner they learn!

Dynamic Stretching!

DO THIS!

Did you know that static stretching before an event can actually decrease performance? Did you know that static stretching hasn't been shown to be effective in injury prevention before practice or games? The best way to get ready for movement is to do movements that mimic your athletic movements in a slower controlled environment. Try these out!

10 yards

Walk on your toes, walk back on your heels (stretching calves, shins)

Straight leg out, heel down, toe up, reach out and down your leg to stretch hamstring and calves, jog back

Pull knees up and hug into chest, walk forward and alternate legs, jog back

Jog with arm circles going forward, jog back with arm circles the other way

Skip with high knees, come back with heels to butt kicks

Side lunge, alternate turn side lunge the other way, jog back

Karaoke, jog back

Hold partner and swing leg side to side to open up hips

Do a progressive run – start jogging, increase speed slowly while moving forward until at full sprint at the end. Repeat

NOT THAT!

Static stretch, bouncing stretches, hard starts to running before fully warmed up, not enough movement to get warm in cooler weather. (Remember those big stretching circles where we count together, time to let those go…)

Did you know?! Hydration troubles hamper performance and recovery! Many kids don't even bring water to practice and rarely drink it at home. Water breaks are not only healthy and nice to have, they actually will increase your athletes' ability to reach their speed, mental, and muscular performances. Make bringing water mandatory or fill up a jug for kids to pour from at practice. Hmmm..Sounds like a great time for some water!! (don't forget coaches need water too!)

Passing, Catching, Ground Balls

DO THIS!

3 person continuous passing lines. First person runs to cone, pivots and cuts back asking for the ball either on the ground or in the air. 2nd person in line has the ball, gives it to the cutter and then immediately starts to head to the cone. The first person receives the ball and passes it to the third person in line. Run through any type of passing, ground balls, etc and emphasize doing everything on the move.

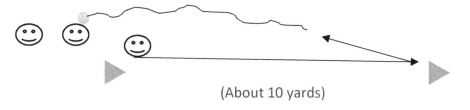

(About 10 yards)

NOT THAT!

 LONG shuttle lines, running long distances to each other, or standing still and passing back and forth. These aren't game-like and encourage bad habits of stopping or slowing down to catch or throw. The above activity is tiring, involves cutting, moving, communicating, and moving through their catch and throw while maximizing the amount of touches on the ball in a short amount of time.

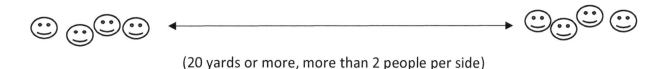

(20 yards or more, more than 2 people per side)

COACH THIS...NOT THAT!

COACH THIS!!	NOT THAT!
Stick Targets in the goal! Place extra sticks from the back of the goal with the handles slid down into a square of net. The head will remain sticking up on the back of the net. When you hit a stick while shooting it will pop out of the net for instant gratification!	Hector, or nothing in the goal.
Or a Giant Trash Can! Most fields have trash cans around, drag on into the net!	Empty Goal.
2 Person Wall ball! One thrower in front, receiver in back. Throw and your partner has to catch it, while they throw it you drop behind them to become the receiver.	1 Person Wall Ball.
Land Mine Tag! Just like sharks and minnows, there are minors chasing a group of players trying to cross the field. Add in players placed around the field that can only take 2 steps in every direction trying to knock your ball loose if you expose it while crossing. Try to cradle through the landmine while avoiding being tagged by the Miners, but watch out for those shifting landmines too, they're trying to take your treasure!	Running and Craddling.
Catching and Shooting with PRESSURE! Start at the top of the 8 and cut in for a pass. Two people behind you at the 12 are racing in to check your hanging stick or put pressure on either side of you and rush you to shoot. Rotate lines every time so everyone plays D, feeds, and shoots.	Feeding and shooting with no pressure and a long line.
Tennis Balls or SWAX Balls for close in shots, crease rolls, one v ones, or 8 meters.	Regular balls pelted at the goalie! YIKES!

EASY STATIONS:

1. **ONE V ONE tag the cone drill.** Put out a line of cones. Two players per cone. One player is protecting and boxing out the cone, the other is trying to tag it with their hand. 30 seconds they try to get the cone and then they switch roles.

2. **Mirror Drill:** Two players going against each other. One is offense and other is defense. They face each other about a stick length apart. Offense can move forward, backward or side to side within a small area. Defense must stay within a stick length and not be fooled by the offense quick movements and changes of direction. Make it harder – have the players hold a piece of streamer that is about 8 feet long, defense - don't let the streamer break, stay with them.

3. **Continuous Pick and Pass**: (requires knowledge of setting picks before running this drill) Set up a box, one offense player at each cone. Player passes the ball and then goes to set a pick at another cone. Player who has pick set for them runs off it and cuts to receive ball and takes it to the empty cone spot. They then pass it and go set a pick. Progress it: Use pick and then person who sets pick rolls off and gets the ball back. Progress it again: Add defense that plays at 50%.

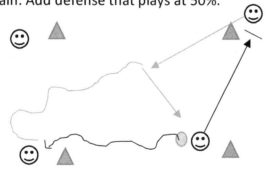

4. **52 Pick up.** 3 players in a triangle (cones about 5 yards apart) Roll the ball to a cone, a player who is not already at that cone must run there and pick it up and then roll it to another cone where someone else must run to get it. Keep moving the ball and scooping it until you've picked it up 52 times. Racing other groups of 3 to get to 52.

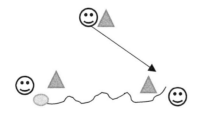

STICK WORK

DO THIS!

Longest pass using the back of the stick. Don't just partner up (unless they are brand new players) Put them in groups of five and quick stick it around, passing a skip pass to their left all the way around the group using the back of their stick. One point for every time they get it around. Make it harder? Non-dom with the back of their stick, add in more balls, use tennis balls..

DO THIS!

Ground ball, find the open player, get the pass there accurately. Make a box with different colored cones. Use different colored balls to match the cones (or write the name of the color on the ball with different colors to match the cones) Put the player in the box and put four post players out, one on each cone. Roll a ball in the box and the player will scoop the ball and throw it to the person at the cone that coordinates with the color written on the ball. Immediately roll in another one, post players should call out ball down to alert the player the next ball is live. Time how long it takes to get all four balls to their posts. Then switch players in the middle until everyone has had a chance and see who has the fastest time while still being accurate.

DO THIS!

Use three different color foam balls (dollar store is great for these, swax balls, anything that's not hard and that has distinctly different colors. Even beanie babies work. More experienced players you could write large numbers on tennis balls and call numbers) Have a partner throw the balls up in the air all at once and call out a color and then pop out because they will be an outlet for a pass. The other partner must track the ball color that was called out and catch it and throw it to their partner who is popping out. They must catch the ball before it hits the ground and complete the pass to count the point.

Stations using BOXES

DO THIS!

Cat and mouse – 3 people inside a 5 yard box. One cat chasing a mouse, one angry grandma trying to keep body position between the cat and mouse and protect the mouse. No sticks, just fun and trying to tag the mouse. Go for 1 minute and then switch roles.

The Last Cookie- One V One inside the box. Protecting the last cookie in your stick! One has the ball (cookie) and maintains shoulder-shoulder-ball protection. The other is trying to tag the stick. Don't get trapped in the corner! Go for a minute and then switch.

2v2 Small box, 4 people, two teams. One team passes back and forth counting every completed pass. The other team tries to turn the ball over or make them drop it. Don't go out of the box! If the ball is turned over then the other team is counting away. Once the ball drops or is turned over the counting must start again. Who will get the highest number of consecutive completed passes?

Open Post – A player at each corner with a ball. One offense in the center receiving a pass from each post and returning it to that post. Must receive a pass from each post player and get it back to them before the players switch. But inside that box the offense player has a defender trying to keep them from receiving or passing that ball inside the box. Learning to get the defender on their backside so they can successfully move the ball.

3 Man Quick Sand (3v2) 3 offense players, one 5 yard box. Two of the players are outside the box moving around on any side they want as long as they are never on the same side together. The third offense player must stay in the box. One defender outside the box can go anywhere outside the box they want to marking either of the two offense players out there with them. One defender inside the box marking the attack player. Objective is to get the ball from one offense player to the player inside the box and then outside to the other offense player. All three touch it and they get a point. Keep going and count points. Defense gets points for turnovers then gives the ball back and continues. Switch roles after 2 minutes. Defense CAN COME OUT OF THE BOX but they must work together because if the defender comes out of the box then the other defender must go in. There must always be one defense player inside and one outside of the box. This can be done with lacrosse sticks and balls or playground ball and no sticks to work on body position and movement.

Offensive Motion and Spacing: (OFFENSE)

DO THIS!

Place a circle of cones in front of the crease where you'd like them to ask for the ball. Call a player's name (or have a designated person start). That person runs into the center circle, calls someone's name and then runs out and takes the spot of the person who's name they called. When the player hears their name called they run into the circle and repeat the process. They should be headed into the circle as soon as their name is called, not waiting for the first person to get to their spot. There should be an overlap on the cuts to keep it moving.

Add in the next step: Call for the ball first when entering the circle, then call someone's name.

Next step: Give a kickball to someone down low and let them decide to pass it to the player who cuts in when they remember to ask for the ball. That person catches it, passes it back, calls a new name and continues out.

The trick? They can't be in the center circle more than 3 seconds so it has to move fast. Try to see how fast they can get everyone through the cycle. Don't forget to ask for the ball when they are in the circle, even if no one is going to throw it to them, flash to the ball and ask for it with hands and verbally. Ready to add sticks and a real ball? Great! Let different people try feeding the ball to cutters, add a shot in for every 3rd cut or the last cutter of each group.

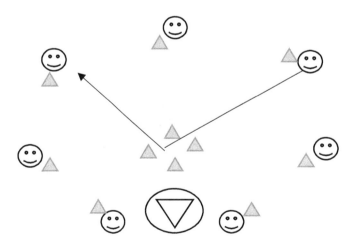

NOT THAT!

Long explanations of cutting, screaming MOOOOVE, complicated patterns or plays. Instead, try this basic balance and movement option in a fun game that encourages competition, speed, and attentiveness.

Teaching Isolation Movement (ISOs), purposeful overloading (OFFENSE)
DO THIS!

Select 3 colors of cones. Let's say we have 3 red, 2 blue, and 2 green. Lay them out in the 7 spots and put an offense player at each cone. Have them pass the ball around. Once it gets around one time call out a combination such as RED ONE, BLUE 2. That means one person at each red cone and 2 people at each blue cone. They must get there as quickly as possible and communicate so they have the right number at the cones. They also need to get the ball to a cone where there is only one person. There will be no one on the green cones in this scenario. (see below) Once they are set correctly yell for a reset and they will go back to evenly spaced one at each cone and pass the ball around again before you yell out a new sequence. Focus on them getting there quickly and resetting quickly as well as communicating and moving the ball.

PROGRESS IT: After you call the sequence and they set up, let the players who are at a cone with just themselves work together and drive to goal getting in a pass or two on the way. Below it would be the three red players working together. Players who are more than one at a cone should move around in their area around their spots, getting used to thinking about being a distraction to their defense without getting in the way of the iso. (the players on the blue cones below)

PROGRESS IT MORE: Once they get the hang of it make it go live. Have defenders waiting in a line down low. When you call a sequence out, it releases the defense who will run out to mark the offense players. Offense can try to make cuts and get to goal as soon as they have set up in their assigned spots.

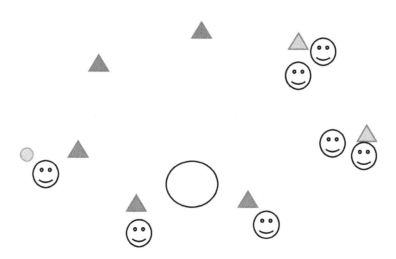

DEFENSE movement, sliding, awareness, readiness
DO THIS!

4 different colored cones and a defender in the middle. Set up a box for each player at that station so everyone is working. Call out a color of one of the cones. The defender must angle their body to protect the center, approach that color cone and break down steps. Call another color, defender drops back to center and then approaches the next color cone that was called. Focus is on keeping feet active, staying big, angle of body to protect the middle and approach. Go for 30 seconds, rest 30 seconds and repeat. If you have less boxes then have two people at each station and rotate in and out after each 2 minutes of work.

For more advanced players, progress it! After they get the hang of it randomly roll a ball in and yell ball down. They have to turn and find the ball and get it out of the box before 3 seconds is up since the ball was rolled in.

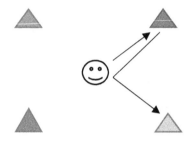

Staying in FRONT of the CUTTER!

DO THIS!

Line them up around the 8 meter in settled defense spots with offense lined up around the 12 across from them. Place 7 colored cones inside the 8 meter towards the center in a cluster. Each offense player is trying to touch each cone at least once to get a point. They can drive in whenever they are ready though they should try not to all cut at once. The offense players get 3 seconds to try to get to a cone and touch it with their foot once inside the 8 meter before having to be back out to their spot. That means they have to drive and dodge hard to get in there. Every time they drive in they have to go for a different cone. Defense must read when they will try to get in and stay in front of them denying their access to whatever cone they are trying to get too. If the offense runs out of time and has to leave without touching a cone then the defense gets the point for every time they foil their players plans to get to a cone.

Defense Communication and Readiness:

DO THIS!

Set up the offense in 7 spots around the 12 meter with a ball. Have defense muddle up in front of the crease all facing the inside. The offense will pass the ball around the outside counting to 7. When defense hears seven they are released to each hustle as fast as they can and go mark a player. Once defense gets to the 8 meter the offense is live and can cut or go to goal. You can set up parameters such as there must be a double team on the ball, or that the offense must drive first and defense needs to crash immediately after marking up, etc. Use what you need to focus on most as your objective and pick one thing at a time to look at and work on and let the other stuff go.

DO THIS!

Play 7v7 around the attack area. As you are playing yell FIRE and whoever has the ball has to chuck it out of bounds as a new ball rolls into the 8 meter for a ground ball battle and either defensive clear or offensive repossession.

DO THIS!

3v3 CHAOS drill teaches communicating and decision making when caught out of position with a driving offense. Ball starts with a pass which makes the play go live. Defense must decide to go man, double team, avoid shooting space and cut off passing lanes. Offense needs to move the ball quickly, drive hard and find the option before defense figures out the chaos.

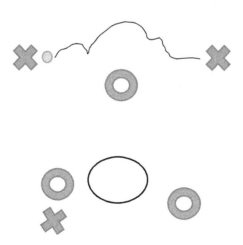

5v4 Slide from the back Side (defense communication, movement, readiness and offense ball movement and reading defenders)

DO THIS!

Set up 5 cones (box and one in the middle) about 15 yards across. One attacker at every cone so that you have 5 total on offense. 4 Defenders – one on ball, one on each adjacent and one sliding to cover the middle. The objective for offense is to get the ball to the person in the middle and get the ball back to score a point. Defense must shift as the ball moves to cover ball and adjacents to deny the pass and leave the girl farthest from ball open. Defense must learn to move while the ball is in the air, anticipating rather than reacting. Start with a playground ball and no sticks. (below, defense is the green lightning bolt, on ball side to deny pass. Middle defender is also looking to knock down the long pass overhead and will shift as ball is in the air if the pass is being made. The defender on ball would then shift forward to cover middle OR would shift to cover an open adjacent if one of those defender leaves to take middle.) It's all about shifting quickly, moving to stick side and with sticks in the passing lanes while communicating.)

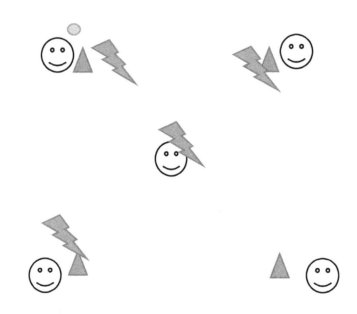

Falling back to the 8 (DEFENSE) (also known as, what to do when you're getting clobbered and your defense is getting burned out wide)

DO THIS!

Make a large box about 20 yards wide. Make a smaller box, about 10 yards, inside of the larger box. Have offense players work the ball around the outside of the box and defense mark tightly trying to deny passes and force passes clockwise. Yell DROP and have defense rush back to the smaller box to defend it. Yell attack and allow attackers to drive and try to get inside the box to tag a cone in the middle. Defense is working on staying in front of cutters, crashing, doubling and denying the middle. Call for attackers to reset back around the larger box, defense should stay on the smaller box. Call attack again and they will redrive in testing the defense commitment to protect the middle and not follow out.

Progress it by going to full 7v7 using the 12 and the 8 instead of the boxes.

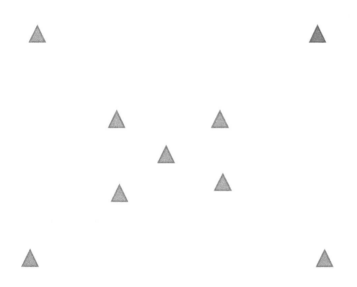

Thread the Needle

DO THIS!

Set up 2 offense players inside the 8 meter. Put 5 to 7 more offense players spread out all the way around the 12. (this can also be done with cone boxes if you need to do it without lined area)

Tell the rest of the players in the drill that they are defense and to spread out around the 8 meter facing the offense players with their sticks up. They are trying to deny any passes from getting into the two offense players inside the 8. The defense can go anywhere in between the area that is between the 8m and the 12 meter but they cannot go into the 8 or past the 12. The players around the outside have two balls they are working around and trying to get to their two players inside the 8 without being intercepted. They get points every time the ball gets to their players and then sent back out to them and caught. Defense gets a point for every knock down they get possession of or interception, then they give the ball back to offense and keep going.

Let the goalie go in the cage to help defense. Goalie can go anywhere inside the crease and try to knock down passes as well.

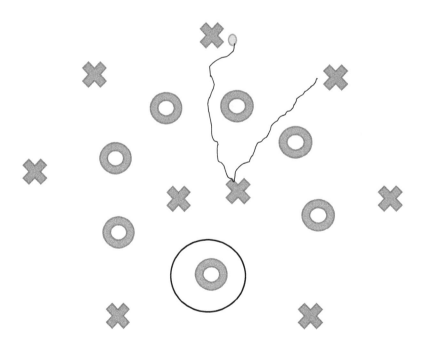

The Draw Drill (MIDFIELD)

DO THIS!

Practice your 3 man middie game in a station! Can be done in any size box to shrink down the area and make it tight space for moving, cutting, and popping out.

Set up 3 cones. At the center cone throw the ball up in the air where the two centers will try to get possession. At the other two cones the middies will be told to either deny pass, double the ball, pop out for a pass or drop to protect defensive side of the box. It's ok if this is a smaller scale, the concept is what's important. You can use lacrosse sticks and balls or playground balls and focus just on movement and spacing. Pick ONE focus at a time (double team/pop out/box out, etc) This is just a mini real game draw, but by changing the size of the box you teach wining the ball under more pressure. Try adding an extra person or two on defense running in from the sidelines to teach beating extra pressure so the real game scenario feels easy.

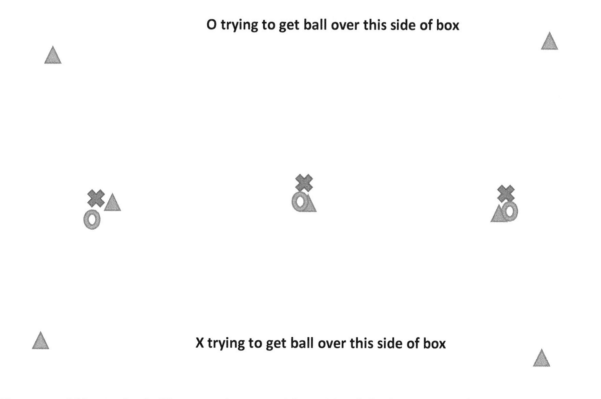

O trying to get ball over this side of box

X trying to get ball over this side of box

You can add in marked offense options on either side of the box as well for possible outlets but they are not allowed to enter the box, only offer support from the outside of their line.

MIDFIELD Transition (head up, communicate, move the ball, speed)

Find the open person, move the ball, cut, and get down field as fast as you can! Start off with two lines. 3 people on the left side of the field, each with a ball and 3 people on the right side without balls. They are all 6 on the same team, working together. On the whistle, they are trying to get all 3 balls down and shot on the goal at the other end of the field. They have 3 seconds to get rid of the ball after they get possession of it, and cannot pass with the same person more than once at a time. Make a point to encourage them to spread the field, change levels with who they are throwing with, change sides after throwing, etc. Make it game-like.

Hints: If you don't have the ball, cut back toward someone with the ball and ask for it. If you have the ball, look for someone who is about to pass and then call for them to cut back to you. Keep moving!

How to make them move quickly? Time it! Each group is racing for the fastest time to get all 3 balls in the net.

How to make them take catching the ball seriously? Add a second to their time for each time the ball hits the ground.

Working the Face Guard into an ISO

When face guarded, a player may feel unable to contribute to the offensive unit other than taking that defender out of the play. Get that player back into action by setting them up on the stick side of the ball carrier. Because the face guarding defender can't slide, you provide an iso without it looking obvious and allow the ball carrier to either get to goal or tempt the face guarder to drop off your dangerous player. Have other players clear through and let the 2 man game with no slide work it's magic.

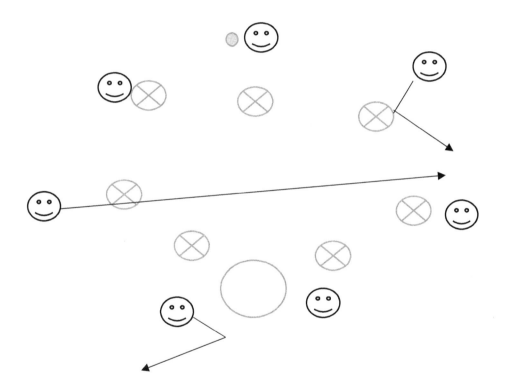

Off Ball Offense Concepts

Players who don't have the ball on offense must keep their defense busy, test them constantly to see when they turn their heads and get that defense to get distracted from the ball. Set up drills that work specifically on reading the defense.

TEACH CRITICAL THINKING SKILLS: Hand out strips of paper that are in a bag. Each paper should have a different action that the defense must act out. It may be that they always leave to double team too early, they turn their head to watch the ball every time it moves, don't mark up after the first drive allowing for the redrive scoring opportunity, mark behind the cutter instead of out in front. The offense must test test test and try to figure out what it is that their defender is doing and how to beat it. Once they think they have it figured out they can guess.

THE MAGNET!

Want your defense to look at you? Moving back and forth while far away doesn't require much attention. Run at your defender and then in the opposite direction of the ball and the defender has no choice but to turn their attention away from your ball carrier getting ready to take the drive.

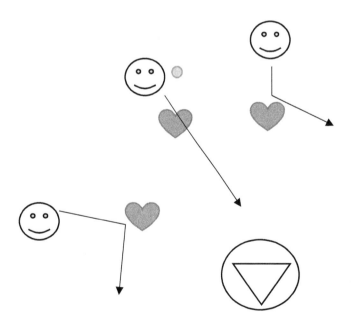

Cut in a V, Make Space in a Line

Rather than choreographing movement on offense, give them a basic set of rules that open up space and get them working together. You learned magnet in the last drill, the art of running to a defender to get them to watch you and then pulling them away from the ball. Here's a few more:

If you're next to the ball, cut all the way through in a line to make a lane for the ball carrier to drive into toward goal.

If you are two away from ball, Magnet your defender and pull them away.

If you are flashing to the center as feed option, don't go more than ¼ way in, curl out if you aren't open or in a usable passing lane.

Cut twice. If you clear all the way through, start to slow down as you approach the other side, plant and pivot hard to get your defender on your back and accelerate back in for a feed. Abide by the ¼ rule. If you aren't a usable option, curl back out and leave that driving space.

If you have the ball, use the space being cleared and drive, look for your options if you get crashed on before you can get a shot off and then pull out like you're being towed on a rope out of the 8 and look for the re-drive, and then if not there, the outlet pass. After the outlet pass, the movement starts again.

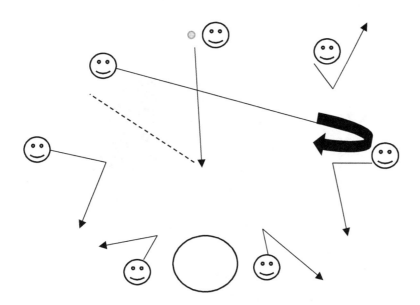

Shooting on the MOOOOVE

Scoop up that ground ball on the move, then off to goal. Don't let the parachute touch the ground all the way through the shot. Curl back to your teammates and hustle back to the line. Exchange parachutes with someone and keep going until your pile of balls is all in the net and your team wins!

Steal the Bacon * GIANT SIZE

Two teams, everyone has a number. Call out even groups of 2, 4 ,6, or 8 numbers at a time. You can't come join the fun until you pair with another number that was called and make a giant by carrying them piggy back. The top person holds the stick, the bottom person carries the weight and runs! You can pass, scoop, shoot and play defense, but if you fall down you must get back up into piggy back again to play!

Make your own CHUMASH GOAL!

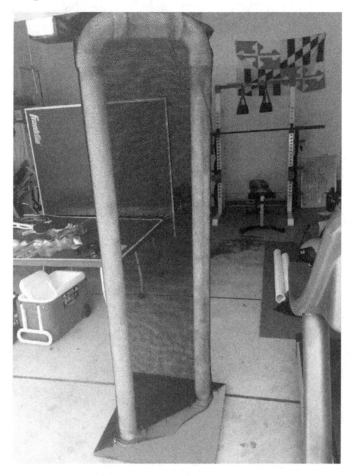

Easy and fun, these fast-paced gems make small sided games a piece of cake! No goalie needed, one team shoots on the red side and the other shoots on the black side. I found directions to create this online, and the rules are there as well. Though- we like to make up our own rules.

3v3 up to 5v5 inside a large circle with this in the middle. Every time there's a shot we have the shooting team send a player off, and a new player runs in with a new ball.

Great for summer, indoor practices, or just something different that gets them thinking about moving and scoring fast.

Cutting and Moving

Pylons, ladders, and Agility Poles laid out around the field in an obstacle course where players will weave, dodge, change paths, change levels, duck, move their shoulders, even have random areas where people are assigned to try to tag you or shoot water balloons at you as you move through. Get creative and get them moving, cutting, and navigating to open space through chaos.

MORE Favorite Coaching TOOLS!

Tennis balls

Dodge Balls or Kick Balls

SWAX Balls

Pinky Balls

Running Parachutes

Agility Poles or Pylons

Swimming Noodles

Beanie baby-like soft toys

Radar Speed Gun

Variety of Colored Cones

IPAD (record a play and show it back to them immediately)

Hoola Hoops

Chalk (create lines on any paved surface)

White Board and Markers

Magnets for whiteboard to show movement

Colored Stickers for grouping and rewards

Chumash Goal

Imagination!

Adjust THIS...Not That! (Understanding your pocket)

The flatter and wider this is, the easier it is to scoop ground balls, but not as good for shooting. Also turn it sideways, if the top of the head is bent upwards than you have a scooping advantage because you don't have to get as low.

These strings are woven around the foundation runners. If you pull on them in this area it will loosen them where you want the ball to sit, in the sweet spot – and it will tighten them where you want the ball to roll and move freely. It's a quick way to make your pocket more user friendly without restringing it.

If the ball is throwing low or you hear something hitting the plastic when you throw, tighten these upper shooting strings.

The width in the middle of the head determines ball movement- wider is great for interceptions, narrow is better for ball control, especially while being checked or under intense pressure but is harder to catch with.

Adjust these strings only if adjusting the side runners doesn't make it tight enough. You want the slack to be in the middle to track the ball (and keep you from having a flat shovel of a pocket)

Adjust these strings first to tighten pocket. This provides a nice track to keep the ball in the center.

Dear Coaches,

Closing THOUGHTS...............

Regress and progress drills to your team's skill level. Let them do, try, fail, and then try to tell you WHY they think it didn't or did work –

... before you fix.

The faster you transition from activity to activity, the less lines you have, the less words you use, the more efficient your practice. They get 10 fold more out of doing then listening.

They don't have to make the drill look pretty to get something out of it. The longer the drill runs the more it will fall apart. Make it short, with a singular focus, repeat it at the next practice.

Be spontaneous, have fun, they will reflect what you bring. Put on a happy face – fake it til you make it – you GET to make a difference in these crazy kooky kids lives, win or lose you're making memories that will last them (and you!) a lifetime!

But most of all..**THANK YOU**! You aren't in it for the pay, the appreciation, the hours, the weather conditions, or the perks (unless your program has insane coach apparel!) You may not always feel like you're making a difference, but you are doing something so incredibly important. Coaches are often the most or even only positive reinforcement a kid gets. That's priceless. Thanks for all you do, put up with, struggle through, and triumph through.

You, my friend, are a superhero!

Yours Truly,

Kate Leavell

Relationships are the foundation of every successful team. Build relationships, and there will be no limits to where you can go and how much you can gain from your experience together!

Team Success System

Higher
Performance

Build Your CORE:
Relationship

TRUST

BELIEF

OWNERSHIP

CONNECTION

CARING

FAITH

Unrelenting
Grit

Solid
Dedication

www.kateleavell.com